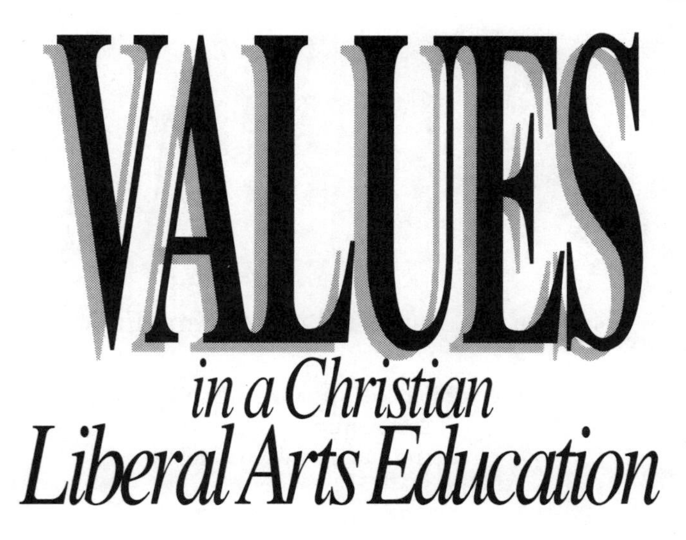

VALUES in a Christian Liberal Arts Education

An Examination of
Grace College's Liberal Arts Values
and How They Are Integrated
into the Educational Process

Edited by James E. Bowling and Joel B. Curry

VALUES IN A CHRISTIAN LIBERAL ARTS EDUCATION

200 Seminary Drive
Winona Lake, Indiana 46590

ISBN: 0-88469-233-7

Published by BMH Books, Winona Lake, Indiana.

Printed in the United States of America by Evangel Press.

Dedicated
to the students of Grace College—
men and women whose values
will help to shape the future.

Contributors

Anthony J. Avallone, M.B.A.
Associate Professor of Business

James E. Bowling, Ph.D.
Professor of Education
Chairman, Division of Education

Paul Bowman, B.A.
Instructor in Foreign Languages
Acting Chairman, Modern Foreign Languages & Linguistics Department

Jean L. Coverstone, M.A.
Professor of Art, Emeritus

Allyn P. Decker, M.A.B.C.
Assistant Professor of Communications
Chairman, Communications Department

Donald B. DeYoung, Ph.D.
Professor of Physics
Chairman, Physical Science Department

Ardis Faber, M.M.
Assistant Professor of Music

David French, M.S.A.
Instructor in Art

Theodore A. Hildebrandt, Th.D.
Professor of Biblical Studies
Chairman, Division of Religion & Philosophy

Jesse D. Humberd, Ph.D.
Professor of Science and Mathematics, Emeritus

Darrell L. Johnson, Ph.D.
Professor of Physical Education
Chairman, Health & Physical Education Department

Edgar J. Lovelady, Ph.D.
Professor of English, Greek, and Linguistics
Chairman, Division of Languages & Literature

Contents

Foreword

The ultimate test of all Christian liberal arts education is not how lofty its self-affirmations are, but whether its graduates can exhibit both intellectual competence and godly lives in a world that is reeling from moral confusion.

Christian colleges of the arts and sciences have long taken pride that theirs is a solidly values-driven educational experience, and, traditionally, the foundation of those values has been biblical truth.

But two probing questions are being asked by an increasingly skeptical public: "Do your students really understand those values, and to what degree do they impact their lives?"

Indeed, in the light of James Davison Hunter's startling revelations in his 1987 work, *Evangelicalism: The Coming Generation,* such questions must be asked of the Christian academy. It has become disturbingly apparent that not only are students in many Christian colleges wavering on key biblical values, but also on the source of those values—the Bible itself.

Perhaps this is a not-too-subtle indication that some colleges have become more enamored with technology than truth. In any event, it is critical that all Christian education take a hard look at two fundamental issues which are at the foundation of its very existence. First, what technical, spiritual, philosophical, and social values should drive the educational experience? Second, how can these be effectively woven into the intellectual and social fabric of the student's life?

Christian higher education has long maintained that it is unalterably committed to the integration of "faith and learning." But is that faith competently grasped by the faculty, and exactly how is it integrated into the intellectual dynamics of the classroom?

Making the Christian college a mere escape from the acids of contemporary thought is just not good enough. If graduates are to live skillfully, as well as work successfully, the agenda of the modern faculty must change.

The commitment to revealed truth as contained in Scripture must consist of more than a casual, patronizing nod. It just is not possible to integrate values that are not believed or well understood.

Then there must be a high degree of intentionality in the integrating process. Biblical values need to be woven into classroom experience without compromise to the integrity of the subject matter.

The intellectual agenda of the Christian college faculty must consist of more than just the integration of spiritual values into various disciplines. Larger educational issues are at stake here. It is vital that the academy identify all the values and goals that underlie the student experience and assure that they represent more than mere fossilized theories attractively displayed in academic museum cases.

The first step taken by the Grace College faculty, under the leadership of Dr. Ronald Manahan, then Academic Dean (and now Provost), was to establish a Curriculum Task Force in

1985. This team developed a set of educational values approved by the college's long-range planning committee.

Funding for the project was secured from two Lilly Endowment grants totalling $100,000. The work of the years following 1985 consisted of the appointment of curriculum teams to work on the issue of values integration in the various disciplines, attendance at various off-campus seminars, and faculty participation in on-campus workshops, one of which was conducted by an outside consultant.

Development of curriculum values also saw an added emphasis on international and multi-cultural issues. The main focus of all this effort was aimed at revision of the general education curriculum so as to reflect the aggregate of values adopted by the faculty.

A high priority is to develop methods by which the impact of these values can be measured while a student is on campus, as well as after graduation.

This volume is by no means the final word on this subject. It represents the honest attempt by the Grace College faculty to wrestle with the really tough philosophical, theological, and pedagogical issues that make up their task as Christian educators.

It is their hope that it will spark the kind of thoughtful discussion that will bring new vitality to this campus, as well as others across the United States.

John J. Davis, Th.D., D.D.
President
Grace College

Introduction

Education must do more than teach facts and skills. Education must prepare people for life.

In light of the tremendous responsibilities toward students in the Christian liberal arts environment, Grace College has a strong commitment to providing opportunities to build academic, ethical, and Christian values into the educational experiences and lifestyles of its students. The prayerful desire of the college's faculty and administrators is that Grace College students will graduate fully equipped to enter the world not only with the opportunity to succeed materially and socially, but also—and more important—eager to make an impact on humanity in the perspective of eternity.

That goal requires an educational process guided by foundational values in curriculum design and content, as well as the social and spiritual environments in the campus community. As a result, every Grace College student is exposed to opportunities to adopt and refine biblically based values in a global perspective, to integrate his or her maturing faith into the learning process, and to grow and mature intellectually, physically, spiritually, and culturally.

This book is an attempt to describe the 13 key values on which both curriculum and instruction at Grace College are based. Twelve Grace College faculty members have collaborated, under the leadership of the college's Division of Education and Department of Institutional Advancement, to communicate these values. On the following pages, they explain how the 13 foundational values have been integrated into the Grace College educational process in the following academic disciplines: Teacher Education, Mathematics, Science, Business Education, Foreign Languages, Literature, Physical Education, Visual Arts, Music, Biblical Studies, and Communication.

The 13 values are:

1. *Shared Biblical Value*. Students should be guaranteed a purposeful and structured opportunity to work out and implement, individually and corporately, the biblical presentation of the redeemed life in all spheres of God's creation.

2. *Critical Insight*. Students should be guaranteed a structured opportunity to develop abilities to make skillful judgments as to truth and merit.

3. *Community Involvement*. Students should be guaranteed opportunity for structured exchanges with the community's social, economic, political, cultural, and religious life. Through this means, students can have positive experiences in applying values and skills to the realities of human society.

4. *Literacy: Writing, Reading, Speaking, and Listening.*

Students should be guaranteed a structured opportunity to grasp a functional knowledge of the English language:

In writing—to be proficient in writing accurately and expressively without flaws in mechanics, usage, or organization.

In reading—to comprehend any non-technical material in English, including major works of literature, and to do so at the national average of 250 wpm or better.

In spelling—to express ideas with force and clarity and to discuss on a principled level the various areas and issues of life.

In listening—to become a critical consumer of media and other modes of expression and to be able to discriminate slanted or propagandistic material.

5. *Understanding Numerical Data.* Students should be guaranteed a structured opportunity to grasp the power and limitation of mathematics and to develop a critical understanding of published data, including graphs and statistical results.

6. *Historical Consciousness.* Students should be guaranteed a structured opportunity to understand and appreciate the contributions of earlier civilizations, the reality that all are products of time and culture, and the origins and meaning of Christian theism.

7. *Scientific Understanding: Method, Meaning, and History.* Students should be guaranteed a structured opportunity to experience the breadth, meaning,

and application of the physical/biological sciences in our culture and to do so from a biblical worldview.

8. *Appreciation of the Fine Arts.* Students should be guaranteed a structured opportunity to develop sensitivity in making artistic judgments about what is seen and heard through exposure to fine arts and music. This sensitivity will enable students to evaluate their own aesthetic choices and those of others.

9. *International, Multi-Cultural Awareness.* Students should be guaranteed a structured opportunity to be inducted into a cultural experience outside their own through foreign language study, study abroad, inner-city and mission-station ministries, and cross-cultural courses.

10. *Creativity.* Students should be guaranteed enough freedom from conformity, censorship, regimentation, and the urge for quick solutions so that each task may include the opportunity to discover new or improved solutions to problems.

11. *High Expectations.* Students should be guaranteed that they will be expected in every case to achieve institutionally identified minimum competencies in all general education areas and to explore the maximum of their potential.

12. *Study In Depth.* Students should be guaranteed the opportunity, time, and institutional resources to grapple in depth with significant human problems

in order to stretch their capacities for insight and solutions.

13. *Stewardship Toward Creation.* Students should be guaranteed an experience in acting as stewards of God's creation so that they witness the impacts of environmental care and abuse.

About Grace College

Grace College is an accredited Christian college of arts and sciences established in 1948. Affiliated with the Fellowship of Grace Brethren Churches, an association of approximately 350 conservative protestant congregations, the college attracts students from diverse religious, cultural, and ethnic backgrounds from the United States, as well as several foreign countries. The college shares its 150-acre campus with Grace Theological Seminary.

The college's faculty and administration are earnestly committed to maintaining the invaluable educational enrichments the Christian liberal arts college provides for students. Grace's 13-to-1 student-faculty ratio, for example, offers enhancements to the educational process both inside the classroom, in terms of opportunities for students to explore academic questions more personally and directly, and outside, in terms of student-faculty relationships affecting the student's spiritual, emotional, social, and character development.

The college's faculty and administration are dedicated to having positive impacts on students' lives in the following dimensions:

- *Academic*—The college offers 50 diverse fields of study, each carefully designed and taught to provide full educational inquiry into the subject, acquisition of knowledge and career skills, stimulation of the spirit of service to society, and integration of the 13 educational values.

- *Physical*—Grace College provides excellent and diverse health, physical education, and athletic programs stressing a physically healthy lifestyle and competitive, sportsmanlike spirit as a way of life for graduates to carry into adulthood as they become productive, responsible, and mature members of society.

- *Social*—An educational experience which equips the graduate to face the challenges of adulthood with confidence and maturity is the hallmark of Grace College. Curricula, athletics, ministry, extra-curricular activities, and campus life all help the student to further his or her social skill development in the context of Christian responsibilities and expectations.

- *Spiritual*—Grace College encourages and guides its students in serious pursuit of spiritual maturity and the incorporation of spiritual ethic that underlies the conduct of their lives. A combination of Bible study, ministry opportunities in the community and beyond, and integration of biblical principles into every facet of education and campus life facilitates this goal.

Thousands of graduates have had their lives enriched academically, spiritually, physically, and socially. They have responded successfully to both the challenge of a value-centered community with high scholastic goals and the nurturing of faculty who are themselves committed to providing models in their teaching and in the conduct of their lives.

The following account is about the integration of Grace College's 13 educational values in 11 academic areas. This account is by no means complete. Rather, it is intended to give the reader insight into the thinking and methods used by these selected faculty members and other faculty in their respective academic divisions as they guide the educational experience of the Grace College student.

In addition, this publication is not intended to be a lofty academic treatise. We seek to communicate clearly to the many constituencies holding a stake in the character and quality of the education offered by this institution—among which are students, parents, faculty, administrators, alumni, and the educational community in general.

James E. Bowling
Joel B. Curry

April 1992

Chapter 1

Teacher Education

In the Christian Liberal Arts Curriculum

By Dr. James E. Bowling, Chairman
Division of Education

In recent years, there has been an increasing concern that teachers for the 21st century are not being prepared adequately by American colleges and universities.

These are indeed serious concerns. There are fears that teachers in the United States exhibit deficiencies in a number of critical areas. Too many teachers today cannot read much better than the students they teach. Teachers' writing skills often are on approximately the same level as most high school students. Knowledge of the world and current events is often very limited. These are serious charges leveled at the people who have a tremendous influence over the citizens of the next century.

It is my personal conviction—as well as the position of Grace College—that teachers for tomorrow's schools must be trained with a strong emphasis in the liberal arts. There are three seminal works focused on the restructuring of American teacher training institutions. These three reports are *Advancing the Agenda for Teacher Education in a Democracy* (1990), *Teachers for Our Nation's Schools* (1990), and *A Nation Prepared: Teachers for the 21st Century* (1986). These influential reports have a common theme: the necessity of a thorough liberal arts education.

Christian liberal arts colleges such as Grace College have an unreserved commitment to a broad-based education. There is a "core curriculum" of essential content, which includes mathematics, sciences, social sciences, Bible, fine arts, communication skills, and literature. At Grace College, the required 60 semester hours of the "liberal arts" help to prepare the future teacher for a society which demands individuals who are able to think—to compare and contrast, to analyze, to become problem solvers.

There is also an expectation at Grace College for "participatory education." The student is encouraged to react and interact in the classroom. Instructors are expected to encourage discussion about, action upon, and reaction to the content. Excellence in teaching is a mark of a quality liberal arts education.

The mission statement of Grace College defines this institution as "an evangelical Christian community of higher education which applies biblical values in strengthening character, sharpening competence, and preparing for service." That mission is accomplished in Grace College's Christian liberal arts setting in accordance with a strategy defined by 13 values. Each graduate of the college has encountered these values in a wide array of courses. The adoption of the values was done with the collaboration and cooperation of faculty from the various disciplines. This venture caused faculty members to come together in order to describe the unique contribution to majors made by their respective disciplines.

A teacher trained in a distinctive Christian liberal arts college will be one who is able to think analytically. The connections that are made among the various disciplines and content areas are valuable to problem-solving activity. Many of the subject areas are able to—and do—influence other subjects. For example, literacy is foundational to success in the world in the 21st century. Biblical principles, as espoused by Grace College, may be applied in business, education, sciences, arts, and other fields. The teacher in the school classroom is the first person to open the possibilities of career choices for the aspiring young citizen. This same teacher must be able to analyze the strengths, weaknesses, and relationships of career choices.

The 13 Values in Teacher Education

Shared Biblical Value. It is important for a community of believers to have a common biblical basis. The agreement among the students and faculty at Grace College eliminates much of the unnecessary tension and underlying friction that otherwise would detract from a congenial, learning-supportive environment. The pre-service teacher is able to inculcate biblical values into his or her personal lifestyle and to know that these principles are in harmony with others.

A biblical world-view which espouses ethical and moral absolutes is needed in contemporary society. The Christian teacher can instill focus, purpose, and direction for tomorrow's leaders—the schoolchildren of today. Biblical truth states that a student will become like his or her teacher (Luke 6:40). It is, therefore, imperative that teachers exhibit godly characteristics and serve as positive role models. Regardless of the educational setting—public or private schools—the teacher will influence students by words, attitudes, and actions.

Critical Insight. In the face of significant societal problems, such as drug abuse, crime, poverty, illiteracy, AIDS, and abused children, there must be in our nation a cadre of leaders able to exhibit reasoned judgments. Too often today, truth is cloaked in the skin of a chameleon, because it changes its "color" to match the prevailing moral and ethical environment.

However, the truth about truth is that it is unchanging, and when truth is applied with reason and wisdom, it has time and again demonstrated the ability to solve innumerable concerns.

But it is not enough to know the facts (i.e., the truth). One must know how to apply that truth—and show the commitment to do so—in his or her life. This demands insight and wisdom. Metacognition (thinking about thinking) enables one to develop critical insight. Asking "How did you arrive at that answer?" and saying "Tell me the steps that you used to find the answer" teaches students to think about their thinking. Critical insight is a characteristic of the student who applies metacognition.

Arriving at truth and applying it to life must be essential goals for all of America's children.

Community Involvement. The Christian teacher should be active in the community. This involvement is predicated by an understanding of the religious, social, political, economic, and educational uniqueness of the locality or region. The teacher can bring biblical principles to bear on the circumstances and factors which comprise the "community." In college classrooms, community can be brought to the students. Resource persons from the various constituencies can come into the class and describe the kind of communities in which potential teachers will be teaching. Awareness of and appreciation for the community is enhanced.

Many of Grace College's teacher education students have contact with community needs through such programs as Grace Ministries in Action and other campus groups. In addition, the education major encounters community interaction which grows during his or her college career through classroom projects and observations in local schools, student teaching, and other components of the teacher education curriculum which provide students with contact and/or insight into community, educational, and family concerns.

Literacy. Of the many careers that one may enter, teaching is one which demands a very high level of literacy. The Christian liberal arts curriculum prepares future teachers in a variety of literacy skills. Teaching is done with passion and in a coherent manner from one who has a liberal arts education. The transmission and exchange of significant ideas can only be accomplished by persons who understand each other. Literacy is a prerequisite to communication. There are four goals of literacy at Grace College: a) to read and to comprehend at a level above average; b) to speak clearly and concisely; c) to write lucidly and to the point, considering the audience; and d) to listen attentively and with understanding. It is critical that teachers, because of the nature of their work, be able to demonstrate literacy on a variety of topics and in a variety of settings.

Understanding Numerical Data. Mathematics literacy is a critical need in our technically driven society. From the use of computers and application of their abilities to the balancing of one's checkbook, math skills are essential.

Understanding mathematics and possessing the ability to interpret math data allows students to remain competitive in the future. Significant human problems may be solved by the application of mathematical reasoning. Teachers use mathematical systems in a number of important ways, including the interpretation of tests, computation of grades, and in the determination of appropriate learning strategies.

In addition, teachers need understanding of economic principles in order to pass on important life skills to their students, as well as to function competently as consumers and investors themselves. The ability to interpret charts and graphs, which depict meaningful data, is important to any classroom teacher. For teachers of almost any subject, a thorough understanding of mathematical foundations is needed. For example, currency uses a system based on 10s, while the stock market quotations are based on eighths. Many scientific facts are reported in charts and graphs. History utilizes time lines—a mathematical entity—to show relationships. Much of art uses line, curve, perspective, plane, measurement, and angles—all topics of mathematics. Music is based on the mathematical principles of counting, beat, rhythm, and relationships. Story problems are concerns of both numerical understanding and verbal reasoning. One must first comprehend the "story" and then set up the algorithm to solve the problem.

Historical Consciousness. The knowledgeable and competent teacher can lead students to understand not only that the march of human history has brought mankind to the present circumstances, but also that the lessons of the past will inevitably guide the future. The teacher is perhaps the key influence on a young student, stimulating the sense of investigation and guiding the application of knowledge and insight to life. Under competent guidance, students discover those experiences of history which constitute a "teacher" for the present.

On a campus such as Grace College, the study of history

also involves the study of God's literal, sovereign control over events and mankind's response to Him as the accurate context of history. In any classroom, the graduate of Grace College's teacher education program is able to insightfully lead students to meaningful encounters with important personalities and events of the past. Those graduates choosing the private Christian school classroom for their teaching careers benefit from a college program that gives them the insight and competence to add important theological dimensions in the teaching of the lessons of history. As world situations unfold, students can learn geography by referring to maps and globes, and political events can be examined with knowledge of past solutions and outcomes.

In addition, it is very important for the classroom teacher to understand the history of education in America—a history which, like that of our nation, is rich in successes and laden with failures. The teacher education curriculum, therefore, includes detailed study of educational philosophies, systems, and methods in which the best of the past may improve the classroom experiences of students today.

Scientific Understanding. While teaching is an art, it also is a science. As an art, teaching is creative, incorporates flexibility, reflects emotions, and displays values. As a science, teaching utilizes research that is related to effective instruction and analyzes outcomes. Teachers pose hypotheses, carry out tests, analyze results, and propose appropriate learning strategies. Students model scientific reasoning as they see their teachers demonstrate scientific understanding. The fundamental concept in science is the scientific method, which is applied to everyday problems and concerns. Scientific understanding is a process, not just a product of science.

Appreciation of the Fine Arts. Encounters in the fine arts give the student access to avenues of emotional expression and growth. In this way, the senses and emotions of the student are developed. This leads to the ability to experience the world more fully. Understanding and appreciation of the world are made more abundant through aesthetic awareness. Knowing the arts and artists of the past are necessary for this understanding. Through the perspective of the character of the arts in the past, one develops a broader perspective of the modern world. The fine arts provide opportunities for the formation of the individual's imaginative capability. Appreciation of and encounters with the fine arts broaden and enriche other disciplines. Experiences in the fine arts allow the pre-service teacher to recognize distinctive art styles. By examining these types in various periods of the history of the arts, the student can make associations between art and music and the creative processes. They understand the influence of art and music on other fields, and the impact both have on society. The arts reflect and preserve the civilization in which they are created.

International, Multi-Cultural Awareness. Since the United States is a nation of diversity in its populations, the pre-service teacher benefits from encounters with persons of other cultures and ethnic groups. There is a rich heritage to be experienced from the many nationalities represented in our schools. In examining the differences and similarities of a nation of ethnic groups, teachers will appreciate the common bond of humanity. Persons of dissimilar backgrounds need to come together to exchange ideas, experiences, and strengths in order to solve the pressing demands of a complex world. These experiences can be accomplished by sending the pre-service teacher into the vibrant major cities of the nation for encounters with other cultures. This is possible for the Grace College student through programs sponsored by Grace Ministries in Action, involvement in inner-city service ministries, short-term missions, and other activities. Personal involvement with other cultures and nationalities by the prospective teacher brings a dimension to the classroom not available in any other way.

Creativity. Freedom to express oneself is a goal of creativity. It is necessary first to encourage and accept the creative attempts of children. An understanding that creativity means an experience new to the student helps assure him or her that attempts at new creative ventures will not be laughed at but lauded. The pre-service teacher should be inspired to carry out creative activities in areas never before attempted. As the prospective teacher develops creative skills, students in his or her class are able to benefit not just from the teaching of creative thought and expression, but also from the creative model they see in the teacher. The art of teaching, with its great opportunity for creativity, is tempered by the science of teaching—the application of research data about teaching.

High Expectations. The pre-service teacher is expected to perform at a level higher than acceptable for the average student. The grade point average (GPA) required for graduation from Grace College is 2.2 on a 4.0 scale. However, for entrance into the teacher education program, a student must achieve a minimum 2.5 GPA. This is an example of the additional requirements placed on teacher education majors as the teacher education faculty seeks to graduate the very best students to lead in the education of America's young people. We expect the highest from education majors, and that expectation is generally fulfilled. The practice is consistent with the principle that students who have high expectations placed on them will probably achieve those goals (the "Pygmalion effect"). The same practice must be established in the school classrooms across the United States. Students who are expected to achieve, likely will. The leaders of tomorrow need to be challenged to meet comprehensively the demands of an increasingly complex society.

Study in Depth. To know a little about a lot of subjects or to know a lot about only one or two—this is the debate which concerns teacher education. However, it is the position of Grace College that students should be challenged with a third option: to study many subjects in-depth. The rigors of delving deeply into subjects train the prospective teacher in methods of uncovering significant data in practically any subject area he or she is likely to encounter in professional life. The data are used in problem-solving activity, in finding connections among diverse disciplines, and in developing the ability to make important applications in the subject being studied. The critical skill to be learned is the ability to know how to discover the relevant facts and answers.

Stewardship Toward Creation. Valuing people and the domain of the earth is a critical characteristic that Grace College seeks to instill in its graduates. Especially for the teacher, the esteem given to his or her students is of vital importance to the developing child. "People are our most valuable resource" is not simply a cliché; it is the foundation of the teacher education programs at Grace College. Of course, these students—citizens of the future—must have an earth that is able to sustain life without threat of the results of global warming, shortages of food and water, and hazards in the air that may lead to illnesses and ultimately to the demise of humanity. Stewardship, care, and conservation of the earth and its peoples are vital concerns to Grace College for its graduates, and among the most important values one generation can instill in the next. In large measure, such values are passed on in the nation's elementary and secondary classrooms.

Conclusion

The student educated in the liberal arts environment has had opportunities to learn how to think analytically and creatively in problem-solving. As tomorrow's teachers are immersed in the liberal arts at Grace College, they are better able to prepare themselves with academic knowledge, discernment and judgment, and the life skills that they, in turn, will teach to others.

At the beginning of this chapter, I painted a somewhat bleak picture of America's teachers. It is a picture gleaned from the concerns expressed by educational administrators, government leaders, and the private citizens throughout our nation. It is gratifying to me that we in the Education Division at Grace College are able to make inroads into this situation by helping to educate future teachers in the Christian liberal arts higher education environment.

Teachers oversee the development of the minds of society's future thinkers and leaders. At every moment in our country's history, the future Presidents, business leaders, educators, care-givers, mothers, and fathers are preparing in classrooms under the influence of teachers. That makes our responsibility and the educational environment we provide for those future teachers extremely important.

Works Cited

A Nation Prepared: Teachers for the 21st Century. Carnegie Forum on Education and the Economy. New York: Carnegie Forum, 1986.

Edmondson, Phyllis J. *Advancing the Agenda for Teacher Education in a Democracy*. Washington, D.C.: AACTE, 1990.

Goodlad, John I. *Teachers for Our Nation's Schools*. San Francisco: Jossey-Bass, 1990.

Chapter 2

Mathematics

In the Christian Liberal Arts Curriculum

by Dr. Jesse Humberd
Professor of Science and Mathematics, Emeritus

Mathematics is the alphabet with which God has written the universe.

—Galileo

Why mathematics belongs in the curriculum

Mathematics is a universal language, cutting across all civilizations and cultures. It has been a basic component of education from the time of the establishment of the liberal arts through the *quadrivium* and *trivium*. In recent times, it has always been one of the "Three R's" of education. Its value has increased as science and technology use its power to conduct man into the complexities and marvels of modern society.

Knowledge of mathematics opens many doors for those who possess or seek to acquire it, and the lack of mathematical literacy is often seen as a barrier to those who have not successfully advanced beyond the threshold of scientific understanding.

It seems obvious that most people today are able to survive, even in a complex technical society, with a rather cursory knowledge of elementary mathematics. They pursue a variety of life choices and careers, raise families, and enjoy success with no evident need or desire for advanced knowledge of mathematics. However, there is always an underlying awareness that such knowledge and understanding is a bench mark by which American education is compared with that of other countries. The present low relative standing of students in America in mathematics is something to be deplored.

It is thus difficult to determine the position of mathematics in a liberal arts curriculum at the college level, because the attention that can be given to mathematics is insufficient to achieve success when the student's foundation may be very weak. It is clear, therefore, that the purpose of mathematics education cannot be to preserve or even to increase slightly the level of knowledge and skill that has been gained in elementary and secondary school. A single course would be repetitive and of little value or interest. The basic concepts of number, operation, relationships, geometry, measurement, and logical thinking developed in mathematics classes in those earlier years have been established to some meaningful degree.

It is generally understood that, for most people, mathematics must have a practical purpose, or it does not have any appeal. Attempts to enliven and maintain interest must fulfill that first basic requirement.

However, for a smaller number of people, mathematics is exciting in itself. Its structure and challenges provide a driving force necessary to direct them into higher levels, and then into academic disciplines which require those higher mathematical skills and understandings. Additional exposure to practical mathematics alone, or re-doing problem-solving skills to solve mundane situations, will have little appeal to either of these groups.

One must be directed to determine other values for mathematics in the liberal arts curriculum, with individual attention and concern for those students who need help with elementary computational skills along the way.

How mathematics fits into the curriculum

In what way can mathematics contribute to the general education of college students who are involved in such a diverse array of academic disciplines? It can be shown that mathematics, indeed, is a versatile subject which cuts across all fields of knowledge.

Mathematics is one of the Humanities. The discoveries and contributions of mathematicians throughout history have helped mold civilization. No subject loses more than mathematics when divorced from its history and the stories of the development of its ideas.

Mathematics is one of the Social Sciences. Business and economics depend on the accuracy and interpretation of quantitative data. Statistical analysis and data processing are ever increasing concerns, and these involve the skills and logical processes developed through mathematics.

Mathematics is one of the Natural Sciences. The laws of nature are indeed cumbersome when expressed in words, but in mathematical symbols and notation, they become concise, calculable, and dependable.

Mathematics is one of the Fine Arts. The architecture and art of history have been developed through geometry. Music seems to be a different method of expressing mathematics.

Mathematics has its place in Religion and Philosophy. There are many religious bearings in the history of mathematics, as evidenced by the lives of many famous mathematicians. They felt that their chief goal was to re-think the ideas of a Creator-Deity who had made the universe and directed man to "subdue it." Philosophers from Thales to Whitehead have found, through the logical structure of mathematics, the patterns needed to explore avenues of thought.

Mathematics is one of the unifying disciplines in the curriculum. Decision-making, problem-solving, data processing, and the scientific method all are necessary components of educated thinking in any endeavor.

How can the "13 Values" of the Grace College general education program be integrated into a mathematics course?

Shared Biblical Value. Each class session begins with a short devotional emphasizing the relevancy of Christian principles in daily life. Attention is drawn to the structure of mathematics as reflections of God's structure in creation. If indeed mathematics is the alphabet with which God has written the universe, it must become an essential part of every Christian's understanding. Mankind can only discover the laws of nature, but to do so, he must invent symbols and processes through which he can obey the directive in Genesis 1:28 to "subdue the earth."

Some attention is directed toward biblical numerology to show both the positive and negative connotations of the use and purpose of numbers found in the Scriptures.

Critical Insight. The student has structured opportunities to develop the ability to analyze and assess values and is given basic techniques for critical thinking in life situations in the 1990s and into the 21st century. Textbooks and lesson plans are chosen with these particular goals in mind. Students are led through an in-depth study of 20th century algorithms and the cultural role their applications play in one's economic, political, and personal life. Attention also is drawn to the "pitfalls" which unconsciously or deliberately are found in statistical contemporary literature and the news media.

Community Involvement. The mathematics program is only indirectly involved in this value. Everyone, of course, is involved through employment and other social contacts daily with others in the community. In addition, current issues are always the concern of mathematics, as its practical side must be emphasized in order to include the immediate needs and interests of students. The problems of finance, life and health insurance, Social Security and other retirement concerns, and community economic situations need to be addressed when they arise. Through knowledge of mathematics disciplines, students acquire practical skills to take advantage of unique opportunities to serve others. Some students are directly involved through tutoring or in volunteer work or employment in Christian ministry and community social services.

Literacy. The four components of communication (reading, writing, speaking, and listening) are essential elements of the learning process. Without these, mathematical literacy would be difficult, or even impossible.

Reading technical or mathematical literature demands some different skills from those needed to read for pleasure or for factual content.

Listening skills are of particular importance in learning mathematics. The exact understanding of data and the ability to sift out extraneous information and search for unstated but needed information are skills necessary for problem-solving.

Numeracy is a fifth component of communication. The ability to translate English sentences into mathematical sentences, and then to interpret these sentences in such a way as to reach correct conclusions, demands an emphasis upon all of the components of communication.

Understanding Numerical Data. This is the obvious purpose and value of mathematics in the liberal arts curriculum. This involves more than mere numerical computation skill, or arithmetical problem-solving. It includes the higher skills necessary to understand and interpret quantitative information intelligently. One primary goal is to reduce mathematical anxiety for those who may have developed mental blocks toward mathematics because of unfortunate earlier experiences. The diagnostic approach to mathematical difficulties demonstrates clearly that those difficulties are generally specific in nature. Confidence in one's ability is the first step toward mathematical success. Then the skills, knowledge, and processes can be satisfactorily directed toward problem-solving, statistical interpretation, and functional proficiency.

Historical Consciousness. No subject loses more if divorced from its history than mathematics. The mathematics course of study should strive to emphasize events and people of historical import, both of the past and present. The history of the Hindu-Arabic system, the contributions of mathematicians, and the flow of the development of mathematical thought from Thales to the 1990s are a fundamental part of mathematical understanding. The space program, the ever-changing voting apportionment which depends on the decennial census, and the budgetary fights in Washington are all a part of history. The development of mathematics is so closely associated with the cultural, social, and technical development of modern society that it cannot be ignored. There are many religious bearings in the development of mathematics to be considered as well. The biographies of many early mathematicians clearly show the contributions religion and mathematics have made to each other.

Scientific Understanding. Mathematics is closely related to science by its very nature. Any serious study of mathematics will enhance one's scientific understanding and will better equip one to apply scientific reasoning in his or her life. Science is the study of things in certain quantities, and only through mathematics can one find the tools and formulas by which these quantities can be measured, and from which predictions can be made. Both mathematics and science have come down through history from a stream of religious thinkers who felt they were interpreting a universe created by a Creator-Deity who was consistent and could be understood. They knew that man was created in the image of God, with the ability to discover and interpret the natural laws which God Himself had placed here. To do this, mankind has had to invent symbols and operation rules by which people may follow after God's thoughts as expressed in His general revelation of Himself through nature. In this sense, mathematics and science are interpreted as reflections of the mind of God, and this should be frequently and continually emphasized.

Appreciation of the Fine Arts. The study of shapes, symmetry, and patterns are part of art and architecture—i.e., the golden rectangle and the Fibonacci sequence. Music is structured mathematically and consequently could be considered to be a form of mathematics. The mathematician finds in the elegance and sophistication of his work an appeal to the spirit which is an aesthetic appeal not unlike that found in the fine arts.

International, Multi-Cultural Awareness. Historically, mathematics has developed as a multi-cultural science. Mathematics is perhaps the international language, and scholars can move more easily from one country to another in mathematics than in a discipline requiring more literary ability. The contributions of other cultures is an ongoing reality. The success of both Western and Eastern cultures in contemporary education in the United States and the large number of graduate students presently in our universities mean that mathematics is neither dead nor passive. In its early stages, the computer revolution grew through the mathematics curriculum and has involved the totality of world cultures. Even very early civilizations contributed number systems—the Hindu-Arabic numerals and processes and economic and commercial methods that we use today. Such concepts are part of every mathematics program, and arise in nearly every lesson.

Creativity. One often thinks of mathematicians who are creative as somewhat strange, and it is difficult to follow the thinking of some of the most advanced and pure mathematicians. However, on an elementary level, creativity can be generated by recognizing that there are many different ways to solve problems, and many times there are many different solutions to the same problem. Students need to be encouraged to pose new solutions to existing questions and to raise new questions. They should be further encouraged to evaluate both the old and the new for possible better methods or solutions to mathematical situations. Creativity is often an individual process, but students should be encouraged to engage in cooperative learning experiences, sharing in their research and use of problem-solving techniques.

High Expectations. Every teacher and every student should approach a subject with the positive outlook that something good will result from the study. Each student should be encouraged to go beyond his or her concept of his or her own potential in mathematics. This involves skill, of course, but it can also mean awakening abilities, appreciations, and enjoyment of success. Students should be able to eliminate their mathematical anxieties and realize that there are many opportunities in mathematics to learn more and to understand more. No one should be satisfied with the minimum competency in mathematics, and there is no maximum limit to progress for anyone.

Study in Depth. A single semester course in mathematics in a class with so many different backgrounds and levels of ability represented cannot in itself lead to depth of understanding. There are library resources, computer laboratories, science equipment, textbooks, and professors available so that any student can study some topic of interest in depth. This approach to mathematics as a general education course provides the common community of information for students of all disciplines. Depth of understanding generally depends upon individual interest and time constraints, and students are encouraged to broaden their interests, as well as to explore something in depth.

Stewardship Toward Creation. Environmental concern is a must for the Christian. Mathematics often is a practical instrument in identifying and solving problems for individuals and society. Mathematics is necessary in creating and interpreting graphs, tables, and statistical information relating to the environment. Some current examples include the problems of disposing of radioactive waste, wise use of energy, ozone deterioration, population growth, and economic and political revolution. A Christian should recognize that the "God of the Word" and the "God of the World" are one and the same and that mankind's responsibility toward creation was given by the Creator Himself.

Conclusion

In 1958, 31 states had requirements for at least 1.1 years of mathematics for high school graduation. By 1986, 45 states were requiring 2.3 years of mathematics for graduation. Although this does not mean that the quality of mathematical understanding will double along with the quantity required, it should mean that students will arrive in college with a greater understanding.

Consequently, the program for general education in mathematics in a Christian liberal arts setting must be a changing one and must be evaluated continually to best meet the needs of the students and their abilities and interests.

Chapter 3

Science

In the Christian Liberal Arts Curriculum

By Dr. Donald B. DeYoung, Chairman
Physical Science Department

All students at Grace College study science in the General Education course "Science and Society," and also in various electives.

There also are "targeted" elective courses—"Science of Music" for Music majors, "Digital Electronics" for computer students, etc. Students majoring in Science and Science Education, of course, go much further in technical training.

An understanding of both the power and the limitations of science is needed by everyone today. We all make daily decisions regarding diverse issues such as recycling, health care, auto safety, diet, and employment conditions. Each of these decision areas has major scientific components.

The Grace College student cannot possibly be given "cookbook" answers to every technical question, but instead is shown how to approach such questions with an inquiring and evaluating mind. That is, a major goal of science courses is to replace science anxiety with a positive, yet non-intimidated attitude. Knowing mathematics, "the language of science," is also important to student confidence in technical matters.

The major portion of this chapter describes how educational values are integrated into science courses at Grace College. The comments will also show how science is successfully related to other disciplines of study.

A new awareness of educational values in the classroom has been a refreshing approach for the Grace College science faculty in recent years. It has not been particularly easy. Each of us was trained in narrow, technical fields with an emphasis on laboratory research. This background continues to be a prerequisite for most graduate science degrees.

Traditionally, science and technology faculty have been somewhat proud of their narrowness and separation from the liberal arts concept. Still today, there are very few science texts that attempt to present a holistic view of the particular subject matter. Instead of addressing this problem of incompleteness, many science texts even seem to be moving away from historical comments as they strive to pack a thousand or more pages of technical content between the book covers.

This failure of science to communicate with most people on a basic level is doubtless a contributing cause of the current serious decline in science credibility in the United States. On the Grace College campus, at least, it is our privilege and challenge to reverse this trend. The effort has led to a broadening of our own individual science backgrounds through reading, workshops, and team teaching. The task of teaching science the "best" way is never complete, but we are committed to continued progress in future years. The following section shows how educational values have aided our efforts.

Educational Values

Shared Biblical Value. In a 1991 *Time Magazine* article, "Science under Siege," the science establishment was criticized for publishing too much biased and sometimes fraudulent research. In certain recently publicized cases of laboratory deception, the perpetrators showed no remorse or real understanding of the problem.

In strong contrast, a biblical foundation of ethics calls for fairness and honesty, whether in science or elsewhere. In class, case studies of scientific errors provide valuable insight into human failings. On the positive side, Scripture is also of great help in discussing origins, science history, the mystery of natural laws, and current topics like the ethics of genetic engineering.

Critical Insight. Science involves the solution of problems, and, often, the initially known quantities are either too many or too few. Students are shown, by example, how such problems can be analyzed, simplified, and sometimes solved exactly. At other times, approximation and judgment must be used. Science problem-solving, whether in the laboratory or at the computer, is an excellent training ground for general decision-making.

Community Involvement. Grace College's science students have enjoyed ongoing participation in community life.

Here are some examples:

- Science and Math majors tutor local high school students. (Grace College gets many such requests.)

- Elementary education students are judges at local science fairs each spring.

- Students have been active recyclers on campus and in the Winona Lake area.

- Local streams and lakes have their water tested in environmental field studies.

- Plans are under way to develop a community nature and fitness trail on school wilderness property.

- Students have opportunity to give Bible-science object lessons to Sunday School classes and Awana groups.

- Attendance at pro-life rallies is a priority with some students.

Literacy. Most science courses at Grace College require one or more written papers and often an accompanying oral presentation. Subjects include articles and book reviews, historical science, current events—all involving in-depth library research and clear communication of facts and conclusions.

We have had some success in seeing notable student science papers published in the *Physics Teacher* and the *Alpha Chi Journal.* The technical literature is studied by students, for both positive and negative examples of writing. The importance of a literature review in science research is emphasized.

Understanding Numerical Data. Mathematics is the language of science. Students have opportunities to evaluate data, to construct and analyze graphs, and to gain math confidence with calculator and computer practice. Laboratory studies involve the collecting of numerical data, and then reducing those data to meaningful results.

Historical Consciousness. Effort is made to show students the rich historical background to scientific progress. This includes the context in which outstanding scientists of the past were successful and the influence of society on their lives. Rather than treat science history as a separate unit, it is integrated as opportunities arise.

Scientific Understanding. Particular attention is given to the "scientific method," including its various definitions, strengths, weaknesses, and frequent misunderstandings. Most courses have a laboratory component to provide "hands-on" experience with nature. Instruments such as the telescope, microscope, and spectrometer are shown to greatly extend our senses. Students also learn the necessity of carefully defining units and standards of measurement.

Few college students have a good attitude toward science, and fewer yet become science majors or science teachers. Therefore we have the lofty, but serious, goal of leaving all Grace College students with a healthy science attitude—positive, but realistic.

Appreciation of Fine Arts. There are many student opportunities to combine art and science. Some topics touched on include: the science/artwork of Leonardo da Vinci, art forgery detection, quality of textbook illustrations, physics duality and the art of M.C. Escher, modeling of the DNA molecule, and early pigments used in paintings. Other possible topics: analysis of color, space art, digital enhancement of photos, and Shroud of Turin analysis. The presupposition of a created universe implies patterns, symmetry, and intelligent design. There are many opportunities for students to employ artistic creativity in assignments.

International, Multi-Cultural Awareness. Historical and contemporary science contributions from other cultures are pointed out to students. Multi-cultural problems such as world hunger, acid rain, and AIDS are emphasized. Science journals, used in student research papers, identify the international teams that work on various problems.

On a recent sabbatical leave, one member of the college's science faculty enjoyed teaching science to third-world students in the South Pacific. This experience brought a wealth of examples to share with Grace College students.

Creativity. Many of the most successful scientists have been unusually creative and unconventional in style, including Tycho Brahe, Isaac Newton, Louis Pasteur, Marie Curie, Albert Einstein, etc. Grace College science students practice creativity by trying different approaches to problem-solving, both on paper and in the laboratory. Students have even been known to find new, efficient solutions! Their fresh approaches need to be encouraged.

High Expectations. We have resisted any temptation to "water down" science at Grace College. Instead, texts, syllabi, and standardized test results all show that Grace College maintains a rigorous science program. We have found that students appreciate this approach if it is done in love rather than adversity. Not all students do exceptional work, or become science majors. However, all students can and should work to the best of their ability.

Study in Depth. The science faculty members at Grace College have particular specialty areas that they tend to promote in class, including AIDS research, creation/evolution, science history, etc. These faculty interest areas are not static, but instead change from year to year. In addition, students have the opportunity to study in depth through the preparation of independent research papers.

Creation Stewardship. This topic arises in many ways: the proper disposal of laboratory chemical wastes, class field trips to local wilderness areas, and the student testing of campus water. The Division of Natural Sciences has twice sponsored environmental speakers in chapel during the last four years. The division also actively encourages college students of all majors, including non-science majors, to take winterim/summer courses at Au Sable Environmental Institute. This Institute, located in Michigan, offers environmental courses to selected students from Christian colleges. Seven students from Grace College have participated in the last five years. Each one returned with a contagious enthusiasm for creation stewardship.

Values education in the study of science at Grace College is clearly a continuing effort. The science faculty have found the approach to be helpful and exciting as new ideas are continually tested. That is one reason why science teaching is lively and healthy at Grace College.

Chapter 4

Business

In the Christian Liberal Arts Curriculum

By Anthony J. Avallone
Associate Professor of Business

The undertaking of business, whether an art (management) or as a science (accounting), certainly falls within the realm of study necessary for an educated person.

If "arts and sciences" is defined as "those developments within and products of the human activities of describing, shaping, and forming (cultural work) of all the realities within the law-structured, created order," then an understanding of business is a credible expectation.

As the 21st century dawns, that which shapes society (and its individual components) like no other force is business.

Just as ancient Greece defines our "ancient history," as Christ ushered in a new covenant, as a pall of darkness draped the world during the middle ages, as democracy and capitalism were heralded in publications in 1776, with the subsequent shift from agriculture to industry, so today business defines who we are and what the parameters of the future will be.

The true geo-political power of the future lies less in military hardware than in global economic integration. The person adept in understanding the concepts, structure, and application of business principles not only retains something of great individual value, but also adheres to high standards set out by the definition of "arts and sciences."

There is conceivably no scenario whereby a person or organization could not benefit by the applications of the basic premises of this discipline. Whether it is an English major, premed student, or someone in pastoral studies, the regimentations that a business person inculcates into his or her *modus operandi* and the way it influences his or her worldview creates structure and an orderly response to a chaotic world.

The faculty at Grace College has decided that an introduction to the field of business would be best achieved through exposure to the discipline of economics. The selection is an obvious one. Economics affects society and societal change. In order to be an effective citizen in the world, one must first come to a cursory understanding of how one's society chooses to interact. The language of our society is the language of business.

A basic presupposition of Christian thought is that all human endeavor is energized by values, whether godly or ungodly ones. As one approaches the liberal arts (and so, then, business), one determines a value-oriented premise from which decisions are forthcoming.

The business program design at Grace College is driven by this institution's 13 educational values. Business is a natural fit, because the Bible emphasizes the proper place and role of our "earthly" possessions.

Consider the following facts:

- Sixteen of Christ's 38 parables deal with money.
- Five times more is said in Scripture about money than prayer.
- There are 500 Bible verses on both prayer and faith while there are over 2,000 verses dealing with money and possessions.

And so, how do the college's 13 values impact the design and delivery of this component of the General Education curriculum?

As for connections between this context area and others, many come to mind. Capitalism and history have a hand-in-glove relationship as currently does capitalism and democracy. (Hence the rise of the term "democratic capitalism" today.) Which has defined the other—is it capitalism defining modern history or vice versa? Certainly economics shapes and molds world events.

This subject area's other cousins would be in the "development" and "civilization" areas. A business curriculum, properly implemented, will allow for additional insights into other cultures brought to light in such courses as "Development in Eastern Civilization." As previously stated, an economic system defines a community and shapes the individual, bringing it to bear on any decisions made by the immediate parties and providing lasting impact on the way events are shaped.

The more pedestrian areas, such as English, have an integral role in the success of this field and are not commented upon because of the obvious parallels.

The liberal arts graduate benefits from exposure to business through Grace College's "Applied Economics" course. Students are exposed to the role of government in society and its impact on individuals, as well as to fiscal and monetary policies that shape the lives they lead. In addition, students are given the tools to explore new ways of problem-solving and of viewing the world.

The world of business is not only impersonal and difficult to master, it also is intensely personal and easy to grasp. How? For instance, when one thinks of AT&T, he or she thinks of an impersonal long-distance phone company. Yet hundreds of thousands of people enter into its "family" every day. While success in business may be an enigma, the keys to success are few and easily learned. The will, determination, and circumstances that blend together for a success story are elusive.

See Jesus' words: "For which of you, when he wants to build a tower, does not first sit down and calculate the cost, to see if he has enough to complete it? Otherwise, when he has laid a foundation, and is not able to finish, all who observe it begin to ridicule him, . . ." Obviously lacking is vision, purpose, planning, execution, and evaluation—all necessary elements of a successfully operated business. The personal applications are obvious. Wise is the person who is well-versed in this area and who integrates these principles effectively into his or her profession.

An understanding of basic business principles can enhance not only one's future job prospects, but also one's effectiveness on the job, in the community, and at home, because business deals with life.

Following is an examination of Grace College's 13 values as they relate to the business curriculum.

Shared Biblical Value. The Bible speaks plainly and often about resources, such as time and money, and the Christian's responsibility for the use of scarce resources. Business and economics study the efficient use and distribution of resources in all settings. The business curriculum examines secular theories of economics through a matrix of a biblical perspective and studies the relationship of those theories to business, society, the church, and the individual.

Critical Insight. The world of business and economics may appear simple, yet it can require the most complex thinking process not only to understand, but also to evaluate outcomes, ranging from the most obvious, the most tangible, to the most abstract. Once he or she is away from the academic world and the influence of the instructor, the student will have to call upon a developed problem-solving model to understand, interpret, and resolve issues in his or her personal life and in the world in which he or she lives. The study of business and economics sharpens one's discernment of issues separating rhetoric from reality. It develops in the student an appreciation, as well as an understanding, of the pressing issues of our day and the merits of public policy decisions implemented to "enhance" society's well being.

Community Involvement. The allocation and use of scarce resources require sensitivity to our communities, whether on an international, national, state, or local basis. Students will be cognizant of the effect of the use of scarce resources and how they impact the social structure, the environment, and the marketplace. The student is exposed to virtually all major governmental economic policies, such as national budget deficits and debt, inflation, recession, foreign/free trade, interest rates, etc. Also, the unique problems of the developing countries are addressed.

Literacy. While much raw economic data are represented numerically, understanding and interpreting data provide ample opportunities for reading, vocabulary building, and the exposure to magazines, books, and newspapers. The student should become a critical listener and reader of ideas espoused in various forms of the media and be able to discriminate in other modes of expression. In addition, he or she should be able to discriminate slanted or propagandistic material. Internalization and understanding of economic data should result in the ability to explain to others the impact of minor and major aspects of both theory and practice in an understandable fashion.

Understanding Numerical Data. Business and economics provide a practical and necessary use of both basic and complex mathematical functions and relationships. Numbers, graphs, charts, and other visual devices make up an integral part of the study and comprehension of the field. Students are required to successfully interpret and evaluate the various methods of numerical data expression that are often used in economics, business, and the related social sciences.

Historical Consciousness. Economics and history comprise a woven tapestry, and it is difficult to understand either one without an understanding of the other. History devoid of an understanding about economics is without foundation, since economic concerns have such a direct impact on the direction of society. The student is exposed to the great historical periods and individuals that influenced their day and ours. The understanding of history helps the Grace College student to understand the mistakes of the past, while avoiding them personally and warning others who are in danger of repeating them.

Scientific Understanding. Students are required to make practical use of the scientific method as they analyze business and economic theories. Theory contains elements which can be explained, proved, disproved, or revised using the scientific method. This scientific understanding allows for the student to make practical applications affecting not only himself or herself, but also the world around him or her. The scientific method is an integral component for understanding the various subject areas.

Appreciation of the Fine Arts. The concept of scarce resources is illustrated each day when one examines the value of works of art and other tangible objects of our visual and auditory world. Beauty aside, the law of supply and demand becomes a very practical illustration of price determination and the role of scarcity in the fine arts.

International, Multi-Cultural Awareness. Business and economics are in the center of international cultural awareness. As stated in historical consciousness, economics is not only the primary engine that drives countries, but also it is at the heart of international relations and a key to developing multi-cultural awareness. Applied economics exposes the student to the international forces that affect Americans and others—forces such as trade and international exchange. A special emphasis is placed on learning of the special problems that developing countries face, including poverty, and what steps are necessary to aid in continued development.

Creativity. Written and oral course work provides an arena for each student to gather and observe basic and advanced data, and then to interpret, project, and integrate that economic information into oral and written exercises that demonstrate a flair for accurate, creative communication. The discipline, being more art than science, allows for unique interpretation and application based on certain fundamentals. This flexibility gives the students the freedom to approach and offer solutions in a number of areas.

High Expectations. Students are expected to move beyond the pedestrian level of understanding and to exhibit a level of academic ability and comprehension that is above the national norms for students taking similar courses. This demands of the student an appropriate amount of time dedicated to the course work and, of the instructor, the presentation of material in fresh and challenging ways.

Study in Depth. The application of business and economic theory(ies) to historical problems requires in-depth examinations of the literature of business, economics, and related fields. The textbook is only a starting point for the student's study and thinking. From this base, various principles and ideas are utilized to approach and attempt to resolve a host of current issues. Business and economics make up a dynamic discipline with lifelong impact for the student.

Creation Stewardship. The Christian and the environment has been a somewhat neglected topic. This course examines the best use of scarce resources, discusses the relationship of economics and ecology, and helps each student to develop a biblically based philosophy of consumption. Stewardship, in essence, is the foundation of all business and economics. Allocating scarce resources to the unlimited wants and needs of the individual and society is a traditional definition of the discipline. Business and economics attempt to model the various alternative methods of selection and distribution, while maintaining a peak efficiency, whether human or material. The student is challenged to integrate these secular ideas with an understanding of the Christian's role as steward in the world.

Conclusion

This chapter has reviewed the rationale for including this subject area into the liberal arts core. Discussed has been its relevance and place in the curriculum, as well as its incorporation of the 13 educational values. Included is a strong statement linking the effectiveness of a college graduate with the ability to be literate in this discipline. Understanding history, current events, and the future face of our world depends in part on a thorough understanding of these topics as outlined.

This, in conjunction with an appreciation of business on the personal level, makes the Christian liberal arts graduate well-versed in the tools for successful living.

What is it that makes a business education curriculum "Christian"? It is the understanding that one must pre-define and predetermine methods of response, of action and interaction in a wide variety of situations. This strikes at the heart of education. Theory may be appropriate and accepted (and acceptable), but more intrinsic matters must be explored by the student in the Christian environment. For example, what should the Christian's response be in a given situation? Would Christ handle this problem in the manner the student chose?

Consider a very real example in the career of almost any business manager—the dismissal of an employee. In such an instance, all appropriate steps of progressive discipline may be taken for the manager to properly dismiss an employee. But once he or she has met the minimum obligations dictated by the organization's policies, has the manager met his or her obligations as a Christian? Has he or she reached out to the employee as a person with concerns, problems, and obviously struggling with some situation(s) in life? You see, Christ calls us to serve people, not policy. Prior to the time when dismissal becomes necessary, effectively addressing that employee as a person with needs could change a life—and also result in a change in behavior that otherwise would surely lead to dismissal.

As one recent speaker on the Grace College campus said, "When a Christian takes seriously that *all* people are created in God's image, it will revolutionize your company . . . the way you do business."

Chapter 5

Modern Foreign Languages

In the Christian Liberal Arts Curriculum

by Paul Bowman, Acting Chairman
Modern Foreign Languages & Linguistics Department

In an age not only when international travel is extremely easy, but also the conduct of business and trade involves extensive foreign contacts and contractual relationships, knowing other languages and cultures has become almost a necessary skill of professional life.

The phenomenon of expanding foreign relationships is amply demonstrated even for the typical Grace College student who has grown up in the United States. Foreign students, as well as U.S. students who have been raised on foreign mission fields, bring a variety of cultural influences to the campus. Evidence of cultural diversity also exists for students as they interact in the communities surrounding this typically Midwest campus in northern Indiana. To a great extent, business enterprises in this region depend greatly on foreign countries for raw materials, services, and markets for agricultural and manufactured products. Representatives of area industries regularly travel overseas, local concerns entertain frequent foreign visitors, and a number of students are employed part-time in local businesses that engage in regular contact with suppliers and customers in Europe and Asia.

Regardless of the student's choice for his or her life's work, global awareness is a needed component of higher education. The acquisition of that awareness may begin to be accomplished in many ways at Grace College—opportunities to study abroad, evangelistic and service contact with foreign peoples through short-term missions, interaction with foreign cultures in our own inner-cities through Grace Ministries in Action projects, etc. For a large number of students, the basic starting point in really understanding another culture is to learn its language. For others, whose global awareness has been awakened previously through travel or other means, learning a foreign language can bring the student a step closer to cultural understanding.

Knowledge of a foreign language gives any student a more rounded education, leading to expanded horizons. Through class discussions, readings, and writing papers, the student is encouraged to learn more about the world and to become knowledgeable about foreign countries. Many times a little encouragement from the professor will create interest in some particular area of the world. The student then may want to conduct research on his or her own and possibly to travel there. There are Grace College graduates today serving on particular mission fields, for example, after awareness and interest were first awakened in a foreign language course.

Knowing a foreign language also gives the graduate practical career advantages over those persons who do not have such knowledge. Many employers seek people who are bilingual or at least have some background in a foreign language. In a culture where clients come from many different countries, corporations need employees throughout the organization who can communicate in more than one language. Speaking the client's native tongue may allow him or her to feel more comfortable than speaking in English. One needs only to look at the Japanese for a demonstration of how important this strategy can be. The Japanese business community's commitment to knowledge of the languages and cultures of the countries with which it conducts business has been one key component of Japan's phenomenal industrial and marketing success throughout the world.

Knowing foreign languages exposes the student to new cultures, different ways of thinking about and resolving issues, and insightful understanding of world events and international relationships. Such knowledge may encourage the student to step from his or her own world into a different world—a more globally oriented world in which the student will inevitably live and serve in adulthood.

At Grace College, students majoring or minoring in a foreign language are required to spend part of their college career living and studying in a country where the foreign language is spoken, because foreign language study must be much more than learning grammar and vocabulary. It must involve immersion in the culture itself.

Educational Values

As in the other academic areas at Grace College, the 13 educational values adopted by the faculty help determine content and objectives of foreign language study. These values interact with the foreign language curriculum in the following ways.

Shared Biblical Value. The student has an increased awareness of what God is doing in other countries, especially mission fields. It is intended that this awareness will not end with a class in a foreign language, but that the student will show continued interest in God's work around the world throughout the rest of his or her life. This worldwide awareness can help draw the student into a closer relationship with God and encourage increased participation in missions through prayer, support, and personal involvement. Theology is not just a set of doctrines to be learned, but a system of values to be integrated into one's life regardless of where one is serving God, and foreign language study provides a unique forum for special understanding.

Critical Insight. The student becomes aware of how people in other cultures think, as well as their differing values and biases. Critical insight into other cultures is indispensable for today's maturing young adult who will play a role in future society. In large part through language study, the student can analyze values of other cultures, integrating the beneficial values into his or her life and discarding the questionable or inappropriate values. Such analysis is accomplished through the preparation of research papers, hearing presentations by guest speakers, and learning characteristics and nuances of the language itself. Many characteristics of the language reflect cultural influences and thought processes.

Community Involvement. The student is expected to participate in community activities, such as concerts and church services, which are conducted in, or offer experience in using, the language which is being studied. Because of one's knowledge of a foreign language, he or she can be involved in community programs which assist persons who are not fluent in English. The substantial Spanish-speaking communities in the region offer opportunities for Spanish language students almost from the outset of language study, including the chance to worship in Spanish-speaking conservative evangelical church services.

Literacy. The student receives a strong foundation in all four domains (writing, reading, speaking, and listening) in both English and in the language under study. This is accomplished through writing assignments, including papers in both English and the foreign language, reading a variety of selected literature from the country of the language, speaking in class one-on-one, and through active listening in class. These four strategies help the student to understand what is heard or read and to communicate by writing and speaking.

Understanding Numerical Data. The student learns proper pronunciation of numbers in the target language. Understanding systems of mathematics in the foreign language is one goal of study.

Historical Consciousness. The student is made aware of earlier civilizations through research papers and by listening to guest speakers. He or she becomes familiar with foreign countries that have influenced culture in the United States and the other ways that countries have made an impact in the world throughout history.

Scientific Understanding. For generations, the scientific community has led the way in international communication and cooperation. Relationships among the world's leading scientists and scientific organizations are often very strong, with progress in the treatment of disease, medical research, horticulture, agriculture, and other scientific disciplines often shared quickly and openly across cultures. At no time in history has communication among scientists internationally been more important than it is today, as the world faces drought and famine, the onslaught of the worldwide AIDS epidemic, and critical environmental threats requiring cooperative solutions. Knowledge of foreign languages has always provided the means of communication among the scientific communities of different cultures.

Appreciation of the Fine Arts. While the rudiments of modern foreign language study may not contribute directly to fine arts appreciation, an understanding of the culture of that language and history of the people who speak it is able to add much to the student's ability to develop sensitivity and appreciation for other cultures' expressions in fine arts and music. To know the languages of such artists as France's Monet, Spain's Murillo, Austria's Mozart, or Italy's Monteverdi, for example, is to better understand important dimensions of the cultures in which they performed their artistry.

International, Multi-Cultural Awareness. This happens in part through the varied teaching strategies used in the foreign languages. The very nature of the discipline of learning a foreign language furnishes the student with a foundation in multi-cultural awareness. For those Grace College students who desire a minor or a major in the language, one or two semesters of study overseas is required. This gives the student first-hand experience in a foreign culture, immersing him or her in the language and environment. The overseas experience enables the student to be exposed to many facets of international, multi-cultural awareness that are impossible to teach in the U.S. college classroom setting.

Creativity. The extent to which people are unfamiliar with another language and culture constitutes a barrier in the sharing and understanding of ideas and concepts. Fluency in another language opens new worlds of creative interaction.

High Expectations. The student is always expected to meet the minimum norms and is encouraged to excel in his or her understanding of the language. The goal for students is to demonstrate fluency, not simply to master vocabulary and grammatical structures.

Study in Depth. The student is given ample opportunity to study foreign language extensively. Overseas training includes course work in the language within the host culture, enabling the student to hear and to speak the language in typical life settings. Successful integration by the student into the culture demands rigorous study.

Stewardship Toward Creation. A century ago, the new industrial world was beginning to experience the impact of pollution, waste disposal, and other harmful effects of industrialization. Environmental concerns first affected communities and regions, then nations and continents, and now the entire world. Today, for example, the choices of farmers in South America affects atmospheric conditions in the Sudan. Nuclear power plant design and operating standards in Russia can result in the interruption of the food chain in Scandinavian countries when an accident occurs. In one acute environmental situation today, it is clear that international cooperation will be the only path to effectively reversing damage to the critical protective ozone layer. Modern foreign language study reduces barriers in communicating about and resolving complex issues among nations in the repair and protection of the environment.

Conclusion

The study of a foreign language is one academic discipline which is important for the changing world in which students will live and work as adults. The globe truly is "smaller" than it was a generation ago, and it will continue to shrink. The complex relationships that now exist between cultures and peoples will continue to expand. Crucial matters such as economic well-being, world peace, and the restoration and preservation of the environment, as well as the continuing outreach of the church through its missionaries, will depend more and more on international understanding and cooperation. Language study plays an important role in that understanding and cooperation and is therefore a key component of a Christian liberal arts education.

Chapter 6

Literature

In the Christian Liberal Arts Curriculum

by Dr. Edgar J. Lovelady, Chairman
Division of Languages and Literature

While the study of belletristic literature traditionally has been regarded as foundationally important for a liberal arts higher education, praxis has proceeded largely upon assumption.

In the course of an overall curriculum revision for general liberal arts education at Grace College, an opportunity for a more rigorous approach was afforded for literature, among other realms of study. During the 1988-89 academic year, a committee of three faculty members addressed the needs of students, society, and the Christian community with regard to the place of literature in education. The course was to be designated as "The Literature of Mankind."

The considerations leading to the design and content of this course show the integration of Grace College's value-driven approach to literature in the Christian liberal arts curriculum.

The literature curriculum team proposed, after considerable reflection and discussion, that the course in literary consciousness be established upon a base of critical literary inquiry, which requires and develops a variety of emotional sensitivities and critical skills. The committee was also committed to the expansion of student consciousness to a global scope: that is, we wanted our students to experience the vast range of human consciousness across historical ages and throughout the world. In addition, we wanted to engage them in a critical way with the consequences of human actions from a moral and theological perspective.

Obviously, there are limitations to what can be done in a single course. In order to focus our task in a productive way, we first reviewed the 13 Educational Values Aggregate constructed and approved by the faculty for purposes of curriculum revision.

Following this review, the committee determined objectives for a course that would incorporate valid literary study with a globalized range. A letter was sent to the English departments of every institution of higher education in Indiana. From the responses received, it became obvious that there (1) may not be such a course as we proposed in current force in the state, and (2) therefore, a literature course utilizing reasoned values, performance objectives, and globalized emphasis could be an advancement in the teaching of literature.

The course was established upon three levels—(1) *Overall College Values,* (2) *Course Objectives,* and (3) *Performance Objectives.*

At the highest level were (1) *Overall College Values,* all of which were sought to be developed and reinforced in the course to a greater or lesser extent. Certain ones accorded more naturally with the burden of literature than did others.

Contributing to the support of these values in a specifically literary way was the middle level, that of (2) *Course Objectives*. Twelve specific outcomes of a literature course for the student were posited (there could have been more). Most of these were particularly literary (such as a rationale for the place and study of literature, the experience of literature, and the forms of literature), but others with a broader educational scope were also addressed (critical abilities, techniques of language, chronological and cross-cultural sensibilities, etc.).

Finally, the third level consists of (3) *Performance Objectives,* which map into the overall Course Objectives, which, in turn, support the College Values system.

In the prospectus that follows, the way in which specific course objectives interlock with the values system is displayed.

THE LITERATURE OF MANKIND
Course Objectives

1. *RATIONALE*

The student comes to see that literature has a vitality and a validity of its own, and represents the perceived experience of life by humans throughout history. In exploring this inner vitality, the student should also come both to appreciate the different kinds of reading appropriate to different texts and to appreciate the various purposes that one may have in reading a text.

Value 1: Shared Biblical Value
Value 2: Critical Insight
Value 8: Appreciation of the Fine Arts

2. EXPERIENTIAL

The student experiences the delightfulness of literature and discovers the range of both the author's and the student's own imaginative powers in the creating and interpreting of literary works, realizing that mankind's gift of the imagination is to be conserved and enjoyed as part of our creation stewardship.

Value 8: Appreciation of the Fine Arts
Value 10: Creativity
Value 11: High Expectations
Value 13: Stewardship Toward Creation

3. CRITICAL

The student develops rational-critical abilities and is able to apply selective critical approaches to the study of literature.

Value 2: Critical Insight
Value 7: Scientific Understanding
Value 11: High Expectations
Value 12: Study in Depth

4. FORMAL (GENRES)

The student gains competence in the interpretation of various genres, or forms of literature—fiction, poetry, and drama, in particular.

Value 4: Literacy
Value 11: High Expectations
Value 12: Study in Depth

5. TECHNIQUES

The student comes to understand and apply appropriate devices of language used in presenting literature—vocabulary, syntax, rhetoric, poetics, sound effects, tone, etc.

Value 4: Literacy
Value 11: High Expectations
Value 12: Study in Depth

6. CHRONOLOGIES

The student comes to associate significant historical and contemporary events with the specific writings of the time periods covered.

Value 6: Historical Consciousness

7. CROSS-CULTURAL

Through encounter with the literatures of non-Western civilizations, the student appreciates the contributions of cultures other than his or her own.

Value 9: International, Multi-Cultural Awareness

8. COMPARATIVE

The student learns to evaluate comparative relationships between elements within a work and between works, both synchronically and diachronically.

Value 4: Literacy
Value 6: Historical Consciousness
Value 9: International, Multi-Cultural Awareness
Value 11: High Expectations
Value 12: Study in Depth

9. RELIGIOUS

The student recognizes the biblical implications of various works of literature studied, and realizes that literature can be viewed within the context of Christian apologetics and aesthetics.

Value 1: Shared Biblical Value
Value 13: Creation Stewardship

10. AESTHETIC/QUALITATIVE/APPLICATIVE

The student develops skills in recognizing the aesthetic properties, and in evaluating the relative merit of a work of literature, by the application of interpretive techniques, and is encouraged to carry over the canons of literary excellence to the selection of reading materials in later life, as well as to experience the shaping energy of literature in his or her own habits and pursuits.

Value 2: Critical Insight
Value 3: Community Involvement
Value 4: Literacy
Value 8: Appreciation of the Fine Arts
Value 11: High Expectations
Value 12: Study in Depth

11. RESEARCH

The student extends personal command over basic bibliographic tools through encounter with library resources relevant to literary studies.

Value 2: Critical Insight
Value 5: Understanding Numerical Data
Value 11: High Expectations
Value 12: Study in Depth

12. FILMATIC RELATIONSHIPS

The student increases awareness of the special relationship between written and filmatic versions of select works through encounter with 16 mm and video format.

Value 2: Critical Insight
Value 8: Appreciation of the Fine Arts

At the basic level of student encounter with the text are to be found the Performance Objectives, which map into the overall Course Objectives, which, in turn, support the College Values system.

A 65-page manual which sets forth the course in principle was constructed, the bulk of which consists of Performance Objectives and representative Enabling Objectives to facilitate the Performance Objectives. Excepting the process of mapping objectives into the college's values, the model used for literature analysis was *Representative Performance Objectives for High School English: A Guide for Teaching, Evaluating, and Curriculum Planning,* by J.N. Hook, et. al. (Hook). The model was completely re-thought, using college-level materials.

As a sample of the general approach taken toward the 12 Course Objectives (not including Enabling Objectives), the issues considered in the "Rationale Unit" are now presented.

Students typically come to a literature course with such questions as "Why do we study literature?" and "What will such a study do for me?" While the ultimate answer to this kind of question is the course itself (or, admittedly, a number of courses), the course in its early stages stresses both the experiential encounter with literature (the informed delight generated) and representative rationales for the study of literature. In the instance of proposed rationales, students first explore and define the kind of literature studied as imaginative, non-utilitarian writing which bears a hypothetical relationship to life, written in language which calls attention to itself.

With the nature of literature established, the question of validity remains to be explored. Once the obvious benefits of literature are recognized (deriving pleasure, broadening experience), three rationales for literary study are developed by student contribution and by reference to current concepts.

For example, through encounter with the essays of Suzanne K. Langer, students come to see that literature is a sophisticated way of meeting a basic need of mankind, the need to symbolize (attested by such extremes as cave drawings and, in a negative way, by graffiti). To quote Langer, "The symbol-making function is one of man's primary activities, like eating, looking, or moving about . . . The fact that the human brain is constantly carrying on a process of symbolic transformation of the experimental data that come to it causes it to be a veritable fountain of more or less spontaneous ideas" (Hillocks 167). The implication is, of course, that literature offers a basic way of knowing that other ways, such as the empirical sciences, cannot provide (for example, contrast Tennyson's poem, "The Eagle," with an encyclopedia article about the eagle).

For Christian students especially, the realization that the Bible is presented in an inspired literary form has special significance. The student becomes acquainted with Leland Ryken's *Triumphs of the Imagination*, Chapter 1, "The Necessity of Literature," and notes that at least 17 different literary forms are utilized in the Bible. Thus for the Christian to reject literature per se would be to reject the Bible (Ryken 22). God obviously has chosen to use literature to secure His revelation in the hearts of mankind.

A third rationale discovered by students is the apologetic value of literature for the Christian faith. Through encounter with John Warwick Montgomery's concept of "The God-Shaped Blank" in literature, the enduring quality of literature is validated on the level of archetypes and symbols (Montgomery, Lecture). Literature is viewed within the apologetic context of evidentiary rationalism by the citing of St. Augustine's statement in *The Confessions*: "Thou hast made us for thyself, O Lord, and our hearts are restless until they rest in Thee" (Augustine 11). Man thus has a built-in restlessness (documented in extensive literary references), which can be dealt with only by God Himself. The "God-Shaped Blank" is the missing piece in man which can be filled only by the Cross of Christ. The piece is cross-shaped, and fills the void of human depravity. The "God-Shaped Blank" is expressed not only by Augustine, but is also attested by secular sources, such as the writings of Carl Gustave Jung, the medieval alchemists, and the folk literature of the world which present similar motifs or archetypes which have "bubbled up" from the collective unconscious. These are literary portrayals of the tremendous need of man to be healed within, which comes from a cosmic breakthrough in the redemptive process.

Thus, without such a conceptual foundation for the study of literature, the student might be left with the view that literature is an optional "window-dressing" in life, and bears little relation to our understanding of ourselves, of our world, and of God's provision for our souls' needs. Quite the opposite is true. The study of literature and other "non-practical" courses may after all be the most practical, for they operate intrinsically upon the individual and shape our Christian vision of our world. Worthiness in one's very being must precede worthiness in one's doing.

Students who contemplate entry into the field of professional education are responsible for the formative experiences of our nation's youth. Graduates of this college will have a more reasoned, systematic, and diversified encounter with literature (course for course) than in so many courses which approach literature mainly through genres with *ad hoc* importations of literary grist. They will have been involved with the application of several of the major theories of literary criticism (and a survey of the rest): formalist, biographical, psychological, historical, sociological (feminist, Marxist, Black), archetypal/mythological, reader-response, and ethical.

In addition, they will have worked through one or more cross-cultural interpretations of significant international works, involving the questioning of one's own culture.

With its thoroughgoing approach, this course does more for students than do previous courses that I have known or taught. Grace College graduates should now have more resources and critical Christian sensitivities than were available to them in past course work, and we look with anticipation to positive results throughout the educational spectrum that we serve.

Works Cited

Augustine. *The Confessions*. New York: Collier Books, 1975.

Hillocks, George, *et. al. The Dynamics of English Instruction.* New York: Random House, 1971.

Hook, J.N., *et. al. Representative Performance Objectives for High School English: A Guide for Teaching, Evaluating, and Curriculum Planning*. New York: Ronald Press, 1971.

Langer, Suzanne K. "Philosophy in a New Key," as cited in George Hillocks, *et. al.*, *The Dynamics of English Instruction.* New York: Random House, 1971.

Montgomery, John Warwick. Lecture on "The God-Shaped Blank." Grace College, 7 March 1972.

Ryken, Leland. *Triumphs of the Imagination: Literature in Christian Perspective*. Downers Grove, IL: InterVarsity Press, 1979.

Chapter 7

Health & Physical Education

In the Christian Liberal Arts Curriculum

by Dr. Darrell Johnson, Chairman
Health & Physical Education Department

Including Health and Physical Education in the liberal arts curriculum is as old as the early Greek and Roman forms of schooling and as modern as the "Wellness Movement" in the United States today.

The educated person must assume the responsibility to care for all areas of human existence—the physical, mental, social, and spiritual. The disciplines of Health and Physical Education embody the concept of the holistic education as they cut across academic lines to draw information from fields such as science, medicine, mental health, disease prevention, chemistry, physics, mathematics, history, literature, and the fine arts. The urgency of practicing wellness makes the study of health, physical fitness, exercise, and disease prevention imperative for the student of Liberal Arts.

Wellness is the deliberate attempt to live as healthily as possible now and throughout life. The evidence advocating healthful living and lifestyle change is expanding each day. As hypokinetic disease conditions become the major health problem in America, it is imperative that young adults realize the importance of practicing healthy lifestyles.

The study of wellness is a synergistic approach to living that emphasizes self-responsibility and a view that each aspect of life influences all other aspects. The wellness movement is based on the principle of the development of man mentally, physically, spiritually, and socially, as referred to in Luke 2:52. Lifestyle management involves the experience, exploration and application of current scientific information about preventive medicine in an attempt to develop a healthier, more productive life now and in the future. Wellness concerns the totality of mankind's existence. This approach emphasizes mankind's responsibility to practice stewardship, as many of today's leading causes of death and disability are related to lifestyle.

The integration of the 13 educational values in the fields of Health and Physical Education takes place as follows:

Shared Biblical Value. The importance of health and physical well-being is emphasized throughout God's Word. From the creation of man in God's image to the athletic illustrations used by the Apostle Paul, care for the physical aspect of human existence is given high priority in the Bible. The Christian must realize the importance of the discipline of physical exercise and its impact on the quality of life so as to understand the impact of spiritual discipline as encouraged in God's Word. The importance of biblical values as applied to modern developments in medicine and disease prevention must be addressed in the Christian liberal arts college. As mankind gains knowledge about his physical being, he must face the ethical and moral dilemmas that accompany each discovery.

Only through an understanding of God's Word can people make the right moral and ethical choices concerning life and quality of life. The shared biblical value can be integrated by challenging the student to deal with specific Scriptures that concern physical well-being and/or athletics.

Critical Insight. The Christian liberal arts student must be given the opportunity to confront current issues in human health and to assess the nature of the wellness movement today. The student also must confront these issues on a personal level and apply the knowledge gained to his or her daily activities. The need for critical insight is imperative today as society faces many health-related issues that are critical to the well-being of the entire society. Students can be encouraged to evaluate their own lifestyles in order to identify specific strategies to improve their own level of wellness.

Community Involvement. The student should be exposed to various aspects of the community through the study of community service organizations and health care organizations. The student must be challenged with community awareness and involvement, because health care is not only a personal issue, but also a community issue. The decisions made by the individual do impact the family, the community, and the larger society.

The importance of individual choice must be balanced with the impact one's choices make upon other individuals and upon society as a whole. Whether one uses tobacco or wears seat belts does, in fact, impact the whole society. The emotional, physical, and economic costs of poor lifestyle choices affect all of society, not just the individual. Field trips to various health and wellness facilities in the community are an excellent way to expose the student to community services and to broaden the student's perspective regarding career opportunities.

Literacy. The communication of ideas is imperative to the ongoing disbursement of pertinent health and wellness information. The ability to use the written word and the ability to communicate verbally are necessary components of the dissemination of new knowledge and the sharing of ideas that will impact society in a positive manner. Assignment of term papers, research projects, and journal writings are a positive way to encourage good written communication skills. The curriculum features in-class presentations and micro-teaching settings, which help students improve speaking skills.

Understanding Numerical Data. The use and understanding of numerical data are vital to the student practicing wellness. The student must discern the significance of current research findings in the area of wellness. New research is being reported each day, and without a thorough knowledge of the interpretation of numerical data, one could be misled easily by individuals more interested in profit than true benefit to mankind. Students should be expected to evaluate current research in order to discern effective from ineffective or misleading research techniques.

Historical Consciousness. The student should consider the historical aspects of wellness and identify specific events or historical trends leading to changes in the way wellness is viewed in the society. The use of physical exercise for military gain has been the trend throughout history. The student must realize the importance of exercise and wellness for the good of the society and for the good of the individual. The student should be exposed to the major events that have led to the fitness boom of today. Special attention should be given to the contributions of the ancient Greek and Roman societies.

Scientific Understanding. The entire concept of wellness is solidly based in the scientific findings now generated in the areas of medical research, biology, physics, chemistry, exercise science, physical education, physical science, psychology, and sociology. The student should have the opportunity to experience scientific exploration as he or she comes to understand the impact of lifestyle on health and well-being. Students are expected to conduct mini-research projects as part of class requirements. Faculty expect them to critically evaluate current research findings through regular review of and critical interaction with research journals.

Appreciation of the Fine Arts. The development of physical fitness and movement skills has long been recognized for its aesthetic value. The beauty and grace of human movement can be more fully appreciated as one realizes and experiences the difficulty of fluid physical movement.

International, Multi-Cultural Awareness. The need for wellness is not restricted to American society. All cultures must address health and well-being issues. The ability of the student to cross cultural lines to communicate and practice wellness concepts is important as the world moves toward a more global community. Students are encouraged to investigate and analyze the health care and wellness systems of other cultures. Guest speakers coming from other cultures or those who have had personal experiences with those cultures from missions or travel are excellent resources to help incorporate this value into the curriculum.

Creativity. The value of creativity is to be incorporated into the curriculum as the student develops his or her own solutions to problems in physical fitness, levels of exercise, diet, stress management, relationships, spiritual wellness, and consumerism. One very real and practical application of this value in the curriculum is the encouragement of students to develop a wellness program, including components stressing physical fitness, diet, stress management, and other identified personal needs.

High Expectations. Students must be expected to meet high standards in their study of health and wellness issues. No longer can health and physical education classes be looked at as being of secondary value in educational curricula. The student should be expected to identify means by which he or she can be empowered to address significant issues in the areas of health and wellness. Students must be expected to achieve levels of experience and application beyond their present capability.

Study in Depth. The study of health and physical education as related to the concept of wellness requires that the student be discerning as he or she studies the wealth of current data concerning physical well-being. Much of the present data causes the casual reader to be confused as to the means by which he or she can attain wellness. Only by in-depth study and thoughtful research can one make sense of the available knowledge. One advantage of in-depth study for the student is the acquisition of critical skills to evaluate present-day attempts to market health products and services and to make wise choices for himself or herself.

Stewardship Toward Creation. The student should continually be challenged to care for God's creation. This includes not only care for the physical body, but also the environment, which has a profound impact on personal health. The care of the environment holds the key to the well-being of future generations. Only through deliberate measures taken to improve the environment today can mankind attain quality of life in the future.

Conclusion

Health and physical education studies are included in the Christian liberal arts curriculum because wellness skills are vital for human existence and physical well-being. As beings with a physical nature, men and women require informed physical care in the areas of diet, physical activity, and the prevention and treatment of disease. A life that is the product of proper attention to wellness strategies can be one that is longer, more physically active, and more productive.

Chapter 8

Visual Arts

In the Christian Liberal Arts Curriculum

Compiled by Dr. James E. Bowling,
with Jean Coverstone, Professor of Art, Emeritus,
and David French, Instructor in Art

Art and aesthetics education is an integral part of the training of students at Grace College.

Through the visual arts, the student gains access to statements and expressions that are important to the understanding of cultures and individuals of all generations and geographical locations. Art and its related studies offer the student the opportunity to experience his or her world more fully. Sometimes, this is a mere act of observation or awareness, although often it may result in new personal visual images that are created by the learner.

The student who experiences in-depth study of, and participation in, the fine arts will gain broader perspectives and a greater understanding of the complexities of the contemporary world. He or she also has the opportunity to increase his or her own visual vocabulary and potential for personal development.

Experiences in the visual arts enable the student to recognize different art styles. By examining these genre in various periods of art history, the student can make connections between art and music and gain understanding about the influence of art on music, music on art, the influence of both on culture, as well as the culture as reflected by art forms. By understanding the arts of the past and their contribution to the present, the student gains a better grasp of the contemporary world.

Judging the many art forms gives the student an opportunity to employ evaluation techniques. In the visual arts, in the context of Christian liberal arts education on a campus such as Grace College, the student attempts to develop a universal aesthetic criterion. Specialized criteria for specific art forms are acquired in order to make sound judgments.

The visual arts are seen as mediums which have expressed religious, moral, and personal values throughout history. It is expected that any study of visual art forms reflects an understanding on the part of the student of these values. Optical responses to created objects are often mere springboards to deeper, more spiritually oriented meanings. Each student should consider his or her own work in light of his or her own values and worldview.

Grace College's 13 Values in the Visual Arts

Shared Biblical Value. The entire world is God's creation, making the subject matter and forms of the visual arts virtually limitless. There is clear biblical precedent for creative acts and objects. God's revelation was given to men in a time and space continuum with meaning in the physical world. As God redeems the whole man, so art forms and production are a part of the whole Christian living in the physical world.

Critical Insight. Students develop critical insight in order to be able to judge the actions and images of contemporary society and its values as related to art. Students focus on the cultural significance of art and its merit as a form of expression. By exposure to historic artistic styles and the philosophies behind various styles, students are encouraged to interact with the world in which they live. Evaluations may focus on the appropriateness of various art forms and their benefit to the culture, or on the integrity of the form and its relationship to the artist. Art gives nonverbal visual statements significance beyond the words which try to describe them.

Community Involvement. Art education majors are expected to spend time in the art classroom in the local public schools, transferring the values and experiences of their own education to others. For all students in visual arts classes, exposure to differing points of view broadens abilities to cope and confer with those whose values and viewpoints vary from their own. Whether the student is creating, teaching, or working, he or she has a unique opportunity in the visual arts to communicate his or her aesthetic vision and aspirations and to understand, evaluate, and appreciate those of others.

In addition to the community involvement and benefits which visual arts education inherently provides, the students and faculty in Grace College's Art Department are involved in the life of communities near the campus in more immediately tangible ways. Throughout the academic year, the department's Art Gallery features quality exhibits of students, faculty, alumni, and selected artists from the region. A number of young people and adults from the community are involved in art classes and private art lessons, and students and faculty contribute artistically to campus and community service projects and events.

The department owns a growing collection of quality works of art, including a recently acquired 17th century Italian painting by Salvador Rosa; a mixed medium work, "Abraham and Isaac," which is an 18th century French work on silk that incorporates both painting and embroidery; a number of illuminated manuscript pages; and paintings from early 20th century Indiana impressionists.

Literacy. Art appreciation is based on researching artists of various periods of time and their places in historical settings. Reading and comprehension skills are important in the acquisition of this information, with oral and written skills developed through required class reports and papers. The ability of students to communicate is a very important component of the educational process.

Understanding Numerical Data. Typography and graphic design often demand numeric calculations or understanding of the process. Linear perspective and geometric-based designs require a working knowledge of mathematics skills. Graphics classes and laboratory experiences involve the student extensively in artistic and publishing projects created by computer in the college's computer graphics laboratory, giving the student artist experience in the highly mathematical world of graphic arts computers. Such practical concepts as fractions, percentages, and proportions also are involved in the daily activity of the artist in various media, with students who study photography involved in unique uses of numerical data in calculating contrast, exposure, and proportions.

Historical Consciousness. History and culture are settings in which art is produced and evaluated. In addition, art communicates in historical and cultural contexts. The student's encounters with the many eras and aspects of art history increase his or her awareness, both past and present. Like many other facets of historical study, the knowledge of artistic expression of the past helps open windows of understanding about historical cultures and events, as well as the present world in which the student lives. The record of the past in visual media provide valuable insights into human history.

Scientific Understanding. Many art media require knowledge of practical science to enhance the artist's proficiency in both technique and expression. Glazes and pigments are products of chemicals and minerals, and thorough understanding of their properties helps the artist expand the limits of expression. In addition, all sculptors must face the reality of structural cohesiveness and strength in their work. Understanding optical response and the manipulation of light and shadows is one means by which virtually any artist can learn to control art expression. The creation and refinement of new art forms usually involves prior scientific understanding of physical and/or chemical characteristics of a substance or medium.

Appreciation of the Fine Arts. This value is stressed throughout the whole art curriculum. Non-art majors receive a thorough introduction and familiarization of the world of the fine arts largely through classes in the liberal arts curriculum oriented toward fine arts appreciation. This includes overviews of historic styles and methods, as well as communication in light of cultural and historical contexts. The student is encouraged and assisted in developing insight and standards with which to understand and evaluate the arts.

International, Multi-Cultural Awareness. Studying the artistic products of various cultures increases awareness of drastically different worldviews. Students normally encounter this in art history classes. Artistic expression of a culture communicates extensively about its hopes, fears, aspirations, and limitations. So often in the march of civilizations through history, it has been the artistic community that has first communicated about the social problems and visions of societies on the brink of key social changes.

Creativity. Creativity is at the heart of this department's existence. In addition to the creativity of expression and technique inherent in art, the Art Department stresses with students the acquisition of creative problem-solving skills. In the art curriculum, assignments designed to stretch the student's imagination are provided, with encouragement to the student to use originality and to take the creative risks necessary in problem-solving. One objective is to stimulate the student's perception and creative risk-taking, which often are the chief ingredients giving birth to new and great ideas.

High Expectations. The department has established performance standards and expects students to exceed them. Faculty evaluate all assignments in light of high standards of quality (creative and technical) and quantity. The process encourages students to focus on improvement, with assessments of students' skill development, creativity, ideas, and effectiveness and accuracy of artistic expression.

Study in Depth. The basic purpose of in-depth study is to challenge the student to deepen his or her understanding. The process also acquaints the learner with procedures and methods for discovering important underlying causes and ensuing effects. Individualized courses of study are built into the program to allow advanced students to pursue in-depth involvement with particular media.

Stewardship Toward Creation. Artistic sensitivity incorporates strong elements of appreciation of creation and its beauty. The artist's knowledge of his or her materials, the world from which they come, and the world to which they will return through decay and demise are part of the process of gaining maturity in the profession. For the Christian who recognizes God's creative power and action, the awareness is especially acute, enabling the artist to give ear to the creation, to realize what it offers him or her, and to decide and act upon what he or she can do as an artist in reverence and respect. Therefore, the artist's ability to express the beauty of creation can have a significant influence on its preservation.

Conclusion

In the wider Christian liberal arts sense, the college's Art Department seeks to provide students with opportunities to study art appreciation and various art specialties in a curriculum driven by the 13 values examined above. Those are important dimensions of education and life.

For those students who develop an interest in art careers, on the other hand, the practice of art has acquired added importance in recent years. Opportunities in the world of graphic arts have exploded in the last decade and a half, as computers have provided the graphic artist more powerful tools than at any time in history. The computer graphics revolution alone has strained the resources of colleges and universities throughout the nation as students seek to become skilled in graphic design and related skills.

Nowhere have the effects of the computer graphics revolution been felt more strongly than at Grace College. In response to the challenges of an ever-greater number of students desiring to enter art studies, the college's Art Department operates one of the most up-to-date computer graphics laboratories at any private liberal arts college in the nation. The lab, which was established in 1987 and enlarged in 1991, has been an important factor in the unprecedented growth in art majors at Grace College.

Beyond the computer graphics revolution, however, is the department's long-standing record of helping students recognize artistic talent and develop skill and competence for meaningful careers. Four out of five alumni of Grace College's art programs actually work today as artists, art teachers, graphics designers, or in other art-related fields.

Chapter 9

Music

In the Christian Liberal Arts Curriculum

By Ardis R. Faber
Assistant Professor of Music

Music mirrors the soul of mankind.

Every society has demonstrated a rich heritage of musical styles expressing its culture. Music is part of a larger context of the arts, which includes music, visual arts, drama, and dance.

The study of music can enable one to understand and appreciate the thoughts and feelings of human creativity, and since the earliest biblical times, music has been an important medium to communicate the hopes and fears of people, as well as their prayers to God, worship of God, the joy they feel as His people. The Psalms provide excellent examples of these expressions.

Music has an important status in a Christian liberal arts education. It is included as one of the essential elements in the liberal arts education offered to Grace College students.

The following pages describe the place music occupies in

the curriculum, defined by Grace College's 13 educational values.

Shared Biblical Value. In Music History and Literature courses, the students learn the historical background of music: development of music, composers, and styles. The importance of music in the worship services during the different periods of the church's history, developments in the Christian faith through music, and the importance of music in the worship services of today also are emphasized.

Many students participate in music performance groups at the college, providing them with opportunities not only to uniquely understand composers' intent, but also to express their own faith and values to many audiences.

Critical Insight. Through the study of music, many students are challenged to interpret musical scores, the text of a piece, to make judgments, and to perform music in an effective manner to communicate to audiences. Exposure to music theory and its practice, understanding of music history and literature, and having the opportunity to learn arts appreciation help provide the critical insight needed as a performer and listener. The student is enabled to confront present-day issues in both secular and church music and to draw conclusions appropriate to Christian values.

Community Involvement. Involvement by many Grace College students in community groups provides additional performing opportunities. Students are valuable resources for the community through the performing arts—performing as soloists and in choirs, ensembles, and community orchestras; conducting and leading groups; and teaching the skills and joy of music to others.

Literacy. The ability to communicate is vitally important in music education. This can be achieved through practical experiences: teaching presentations, leading small ensemble groups, observing in the classroom, working with sectionals in instrumental method classes, reading and summarizing music information in various subject areas, teaching private lessons through pedagogy classes or independently, presenting analyses of musical works and original compositions, listening to music of differing genres and periods, distinguishing the characteristics of each, and conducting and arranging music. A combination of these experiences in music enables the student to use these skills to spread the message of Christ.

Understanding Numerical Data. In music appreciation and other basic music classes, students are introduced to the mathematical nature of relationships in music. In addition, the integration of music in the academic classroom can enhance the learning of many academic subjects. Music education majors and elementary education majors are shown examples of methods in which music can be used to enhance a math lesson, and how math can be utilized in teaching the values of notes and rhythms.

Historical Consciousness. The study of music in history is directly related to historical events. The understanding of these events in history gives understanding to the development of music, art, literature, and drama. Through music history, literature, and theory classes, the student is provided the opportunity to acquire a solid base of knowledge and experience by creating, analyzing, and listening to music as it relates to each major period. The understanding of performance practices, notation, compositional techniques, characteristics of genres and periods of music is critical. Significant contributions that each generation gave are important in understanding the music principles and practices to which musicians and music educators adhere today. The study of literature and history opens up a window of understanding in sacred music and practices of the church in history, as well as how those practices have affected the church of today and its ministry.

Hymns and their origins reflect the style of worship of the day in which they were written and first used in worship. Contemporary worship services include many of these same hymns, which constitute a vital heritage for the church. The understanding of these past practices allows the student to better comprehend and appreciate the richness of the place of hymns in history and their continued richness today. In addition, music from past church eras can help the student to discern and better understand the interpretation of theological principles and the development of theological systems.

Scientific Understanding. The study of music from a scientific viewpoint is related to the principles of sound and acoustics. Through this study, a student can begin to understand the principles of sound production by an instrument or voice, the methods of creating differing sound properties within a performance or rehearsal hall, and the history behind the construction of instruments and the impact on instruments of today. As the technology of synthesized sound is further explored, the importance of understanding this area will continue to increase.

Appreciation of the Fine Arts. Students taking the Appreciation of Fine Arts course are given an overview of music—its periods, major composers, works of art, and literature. A general overview of music in history enables students to evaluate the artistic judgments of themselves and others. Music History covers each era in greater depth. Theory courses concentrate on the compositional principles as they relate to history and the deviations which occur in compositional practices of today. The study of theory is designed in part to enable the student to understand the skills needed to make artistic judgments and to give him or her another avenue of creative expression in behalf of the Kingdom of Christ. Courses in conducting emphasize the importance of score preparation as it relates to performance practices, text and music, compositional techniques, and rehearsal techniques. Communication of one's interpretation through the medium of conducting allows for creative expression. The student can be informed of the various influences which contributed to the creative expression of others and the impact of these expressions on cultures.

International, Multi-Cultural Awareness. Through the study of the music of other cultures, the student can become aware of the stylistic differences of each. By interacting with international students on campus, the student can gain more insight into the music practices of other cultures, their learning procedures, their thought processes, and their uniquenesses. Music helps to reveal a culture's attitudes and awareness of itself.

Creativity. Music is an expression of creativity, whether it be in critiquing and solving problems in music or performing and creating newly written or arranged music. Instrumental methods, pedagogy classes, applied instruction, and education methods classes allow many students to experience problem-solving on all levels of education, pose new solutions to those existing problems, and create new solutions for problems for which there are no previously developed solutions. When a student is preparing a piece of music, there is constant evaluation of interpretation of musical line, dynamics, attacks, expression of text, texture, cues, and tone color. All of this evaluation draws upon the student's creative abilities of identifying and solving problems.

High Expectations. Much is expected of every music student: excellence, achievement, and the challenge to strive to do better. Because he or she is a follower of Christ, the student is encouraged to regard mediocrity as unacceptable. Due to the competitive nature of the musical arts, high expectations must be established. A standard of excellence in preparation and performance is maintained in order to prepare those students striving to become professional musicians.

Study in Depth. The understanding of different styles and abilities or the need to discover solutions to the challenge of teaching a concept in a new way can provide students with insight and skills for any musical endeavor. Students planning careers in performance are expected to not only probe the depths of their own abilities, but also to develop a broad understanding of subjects in music history and theory. In music education classes, students learn specific teaching techniques and strategies that will help give future teachers abilities to stretch their students' capacities.

Stewardship Toward Creation. One of God's creations is music. It is an art form which for millennia has communicated across language barriers, affected people's cultural and religious practices, and revealed deepest feelings. For as long as people have lived on the earth, they have sought and worshiped God in large part through musical expression. One important goal at Grace College is to help students realize the gift and heritage God has given His people in the form of musical ability and expression and the joy it brings to all who participate or listen.

Conclusion

Music education in Christian liberal arts is of great value to the student. The study of the arts helps to improve aesthetic sensitivity for each student and enables him or her to develop more insight into the music of the great masters, hymns, and the music of today. One becomes more aesthetically sensitive to sounds, colors, shapes, and verbal images as his or her exposure to music increases. Exposure to the arts can serve all students.

Music is a gift God has given human beings. It provides personal enjoyment and enrichment. It is a medium through which the people of one culture or generation may pass on values and knowledge to people of another.

And music is a gift through which God's people may pass on their faith and Christian values to the world.

Chapter 10

Biblical Studies

In the Christian Liberal Arts Curriculum

by Dr. Theodore A. Hildebrandt, Chairman
Division of Religion & Philosophy

What role does Biblical Studies play in the Curriculum?

Christian liberal arts education has at its foundation the belief that there is a God and that He has revealed Himself to humans.

He has communicated His character and will in four ways. First, there is a non-verbal revelation in nature that reflects His greatness and goodness (Ps. 19:1-3; Rom. 1:20). Second, His moral image has been etched on the conscience and hearts of humankind (Rom. 2:15). Third, the incarnation of Jesus Christ manifested the fullness of the godhead in bodily form (Col. 1:19; Heb. 1:1-3; Jn. 1:14). Finally, He has guided individuals by His Holy Spirit, through whom He has infallibly and inerrantly communicated truths about Himself. He has told us of His dealings with His people throughout history and given them precepts by which to order their lives (2 Tim. 3:16; 2 Pet. 1:21; Ps. 19:7-11). We believe that God has spoken, and this provides us with a solid launching pad from which to propel our educational endeavor.

The Bible is the foundation of our Christian worldview. During the college experience we expect our students to engage in the process of constructing paradigms which will shape how they think, act, and feel toward life and others. The Bible provides the necessary guidelines for grappling with the big questions:

- How do I determine what is true?
- How can I know anything?
- How do I make choices?
- What things in life are to be valued?
- What ought I to do?
- What are my responsibilities to myself, friends, family, community, nation and world?
- What is fair as opposed to unfair, good as opposed to bad, and just as opposed to unjust, and how do I tell the difference?
- Who am I?
- What is the meaning of life, suffering, and death?
- What is the meaning of work, play, and beauty?
- Do I make a difference?
- What is God like?
- Will the human race survive?

Through grappling with these questions, students secure the foundation upon which to build the rest of their lives. They are opened up to perceive the needs of others, our culture, and our world. These insights will provide a solid foundation for making a redemptive contribution to our world.

Learning the Bible also reflects our commitment to historical consciousness. The Bible has had a major impact in western culture. It has impacted western science, literature, art, music, and philosophy, as well as formative institutions (family, church, government, vocation). We desire that our students become leaders who are able to influence the future direction of society. The awareness of biblical principles and our historical roots provides a necessary starting point for evaluating modern culture.

The Biblical Studies core curriculum helps students realize that knowledge consists not just of fragmented, isolated digital pieces of information. Rather, truth is integrated, and the various disciplines are organically related. The Biblical Studies core provides a grid by which the theories of all the other disciplines are connected, evaluated, and explored. What students learn in science should impact how they care for their bodies and their world. Information techniques acquired in computer class will have implications for skills needed in business. Theories of psychology and sociology affect how one communicates or teaches others.

Likewise what is learned in the other disciplines is designed to aid how our students interpret and apply the statements of the Bible. Literary techniques developed for analyzing T.S. Eliot's poems in Literature of Mankind can be used to explore the poetry of the Psalms. Principles of effective business management help give insight into the Proverbs. Similarly, the Bible informs how we evaluate and apply business principles. Knowledge is connected. All truth is God's truth. The Biblical Studies Department encourages exploration of each discipline with religious fervor as fulfilling God's desire for us to care for and have benevolent dominion over the earth (Gen. 1:28).

At Grace College, we believe that each student manifests the image of God. Each student has unique talents and abilities.

Hence each individual has dignity and moral responsibility (Gen. 1:26-27; Ps. 8). We attempt to nurture their moral development by creating an environment where they are stimulated to ask why, to verbalize what they think, to explore possibilities, to be able to examine various facets of a question, and to engage in dialogue both while in the process of deciding and after they have come to a conclusion.

In short, we are determined to foster an environment where our students are forced to think through the issues and implications of their faith. We seek to nurture them as truth seekers.

The professors in the Biblical Studies Department are committed to making the word of God relevant to modern issues, both on a societal and a personal level. Students are exposed to professors who not only delight in teaching the word of God, but also themselves are committed to wrestling with its truth in their own lives.

General Education Curriculum Design

The explicit Biblical Studies program in the general education curriculum is composed of four courses. First-year students at Grace College take two four-hour courses in which they work through the issues and implications of both the Old and New Testaments. If they are going to integrate their Christian faith effectively into the other disciplines, they must be well aware of what the Bible itself says about the various relevant topics. They are exposed to the major themes, historical settings, and modern implications of the biblical text.

The third course, "Christianity in Development," seeks to put Christianity into a historical context and show how the church has developed. This course also addresses the major doctrinal issues with which the church wrestled as it matured.

We desire that students feel an intimate connection with both their local church and the universal church.

The fourth course is an elective course of students' choosing. Most often this will be a book study, a course specializing in a theological area of interest (apologetics, the Christian life, prayer), or a course about missions.

These courses help provide a foundation upon which the faculty in other disciplines can build as they seek to set their disciplines on a solid biblical foundation.

Educational Values

Shared Biblical Value. The courses in the Biblical Studies Department are directly related to this value. The most obvious way is that courses require studying the content of the Bible. Mastering the content is the first step. It includes dealing with the following aspects of the text: what happened, to whom, when, where, for what purpose, and with what results.

God's character is carefully explored in the attempt to inculcate a passion in students both to know God and to make Him known as directed by the great commission (Mt. 28:19-20). We attempt to focus our students' attention on the two major commandments: loving God and loving others (Mt. 22:37-38). God's love is seen in a thousand of His mighty redemptive acts on behalf of His people. His sacrificial care of His people is climaxed in the atoning death of His Son. We explore the wonders of God's grace, love, and care for us as His people. God's past care is equalled by His descriptions of a wonderful future kingdom He has designed for us. It is a time and place where all is made right (Isa. 2:3-5; 11:6-9; Rev. 20-22). This vision of God's kingdom becomes a transforming and directing factor in the lives of our students.

Critical Insight. Students are taught to grapple with issues: searching for options, evaluating positions, creating solutions, and exploring implications. Faculty members use questions and dialogue formats to challenge the students by comparing and contrasting their personal convictions with what God's Word actually says. This helps them develop their critical thinking skills.

Position papers are sometimes used as a means not only to wrestle with issues, but also to think them through enough to verbalize a conclusion in a manner that is convincing. Faculty members also demonstrate critical insight, and techniques of analysis reflect on various contemporary and ancient issues. Attempts are made to be logically cogent and biblically consistent.

Community Involvement. The value of community involvement is imparted in several ways. First, on a theoretical level, the necessity of community involvement is established from the study of the covenant by which God established and regulated the Israelite community. Similarly, the New Testament uses many images (body, building, flock) to highlight the importance of the Christian community. Christ's example of transcending culturally sanctioned taboos to establish community with those outside the traditionally accepted bounds sets a pattern for reaching out to one's neighborhood, town, state, nation, and global communities.

This theoretical framework is reinforced by group projects in which students learn to work together and to be responsible to one another. Course assignments also have included projects which involve volunteer service for Combined Community Services, a local social service agency. This has helped to sensitize students to the needs of the local community. The Missions Department in the college's Division of Religion and

Philosophy provides students with a missions conference every year, adding a global vision to our campus. The co-curricular programs at Grace also strongly reinforce what is taught in the classroom by providing opportunity to help local officials address problems of waste cleanup, helping the elderly, and performing various ministries to delinquents and those with disabilities.

Literacy. The Bible is one of the greatest pieces of literature of all time. In introductory classes, students are taught to read the Bible as good literature, savoring its poetry, following its historical developments, and entering into its dialogues as found in the epistles.

We attempt to sensitize our students to the use of literary devices (metaphor, simile, hyperbole, riddles, etc.) in the development of theme. They are required to read large sections of the Bible, as well as modern literature which helps to set the Bible in its original setting in the ancient Near East.

In class, a close reading of the text is given. We often explore various interpretative options, evaluate various perspectives, and attempt to discover the author's intent and original audience's response. The meaning of these texts in relation to modern issues (abortion, ecological concerns, justice, war, etc.) is highlighted, providing the student with a model of how to read texts as living, dynamic, and relevant.

Research techniques using traditional methods and computer searches are encouraged. The reading of technical journal articles is introduced in order to expose students to alternative points of view and a higher level of literary awareness.

Assigned papers reinforce the goal of integrating writing across the curriculum. Presentations of group projects confirm the commitment to providing students opportunity to polish their public communication skills.

Understanding Numerical Data. While the Bible does not treat subjects like calculus or differential equations, it is full of references to numerical data. Students are taught about how other cultures use numbers. The threefold repetition of 14 generations in Matthew 1, for example, is built on the Jewish gematria principle. Because the Hebrew alphabetic and numeric system is the same, there are plays between numbers and words. So the number "14" spells David's name. Thus by using the threefold "14," Matthew is subtly connecting Christ to David.

Numbers often are used in lists, such as the seven days of creation, and as literary devices, such as numerical proverbs (Prov. 30:18-19). Biblical numbers also have connotations. Becoming sensitive to the meaning of numbers is an important part of bridging cultures (e.g., seven is often a divine number). This highlights the notion that numbers—even in our culture—mean something.

Historical Consciousness. The Biblical Studies curriculum promotes historical consciousness in several ways.

First, the biblical account is a record of the history of God's dealings with Israel and the early church. Our students must master that historical flow.

Second, we go to great lengths to show how the biblical account of Israelite history connects with the other great Near Eastern civilizations (Egypt/Mesopotamia). We show how modern archaeology has helped us to understand cultural context and customs quite foreign to our American viewpoints (e.g. Gen. 16:2; 30:14; 38:8).

Third, we discuss principles of historiography: Why does the historical record mention certain events and skip others? Why, for example, are more than seven chapters of John given to one week of Christ's life, while the first thirty years of his life hardly receive any mention? Such observations help us understand the writer's theme and focus.

Fourth, history is shown to have a beginning and an end. History is going somewhere. Thus each moment of history is significant. God is shown to be sovereignly and redemptively guiding history to His climax when the kingdoms of this world become the kingdom of our God (Rev. 12:10).

Fifth, the history of the church and the development of its doctrine is the focus of the Christianity and Development course. It helps students to understand the historical roots of their faith. Exposing them to these roots helps them see how history and doctrine interact. Having a sense of where they stand in history gives students a sense of perspective, appreciation, and connectedness to the greater body of Christ.

Scientific Understanding. While the Bible is not a scientific textbook, it does address issues of scientific importance. The creation is one example.

Empirical descriptions given in the Bible are used to show how the Bible has been misused historically to support mistaken scientific perspectives. "Four corners" of the earth (Isa. 11:12; Rev. 7:1), for example, has been used mistakenly to argue for a flat earth. Similarly, the sun "rising" (Josh. 12:1), has been taken as biblical evidence demanding a geo-centric universe. Our students are cautioned about taking literary statements found in the Bible and reading scientific theory out of them.

Science is, however, seen as an instrument for disclosing the miracles of God's creation. Many of the diseases, cleanliness practices, and dietary laws of Israel are examined and shown to make scientific sense. While the miracles recorded in the Bible have come under particular scientific attack, we teach that God's absolute control over nature makes miracles both possible and historically verified by the biblical record.

Appreciation of the Fine Arts. The fine arts are given a biblical foundation, as God is shown to have great aesthetic sensitivities in the variety and beauty that He has built into creation. The manner in which He prescribed worship also was steeped in artistic expression. From the artistry of the tabernacle and temple to the music that was sung at the feasts, God's worship was aesthetically sensitive. God even took care to specify the fragrances which would permeate the air when they worshipped Him (Ex. 30:1-9).

Throughout the development of Christianity—from the catacombs to modern rap groups—believers have sought to craft their feelings of worship into art and music. Indeed, many of the great classics of art and music have centered on religious themes, from DaVinci's "Last Supper" to Handel's "Messiah."

In the projects that are assigned in classes, our students are called on to participate in this artistic tradition by drawing pictures, creating poems, and composing music as expressions of their faith. Recent projects have incorporated the use of the media of video and computer to craft these artistic expressions.

International, Multi-Cultural Awareness. The Biblical Studies curriculum gets at this value from several perspectives.

First, a culturally sensitive reading of the biblical text itself exposes our students to at least four major cultures: Mesopotamian, Egyptian, Greek, and Roman. By design, we focus on points at which these cultures diverge from our modern world. We attempt to lead students back into these cultures and force them to unshackle themselves from a provincial American perspective.

The great commission sends us out spreading the gospel to all nations. This sense of global mission is fostered in the study of the expansion of the early church in Acts. We encourage our students to get involved in cross-cultural ministry experiences, whether inner-city or multi-national. Several of our students have become involved in Hispanic churches regionally, where they must not only be aware of cross-cultural needs and issues, but also speak the language.

Grace College's semi-annual trips to Israel are taken for credit and allow our students first-hand experience of crossing cultural boundaries.

Finally, this department's requirement of a B.A. degree for our majors demonstrates a commitment to having students gain at least a two-year proficiency in a foreign language.

Creativity. We seek to encourage creativity from our students in many of the assignments that are given. Research projects not only must be written, but also must be put into presentational formats. This often involves our students in creating music, poems, videos, art work, and even stagecraft.

In the dialogues and grapplings that take place in our classes, our students are encouraged to think of alternative solutions and to explore options. Often the class is called on to disprove one approach and then to create one which more adequately accounts for the biblical data.

Class sizes at Grace College allow for personal attention. The instructors often encourage talented individuals to explore the area of their gifts in relation to the topic of study. Thus computer projects have been developed where both the instructor and the student work together creating novel expressions of biblical content. Others have sought to translate Psalms and Proverbs into English poetry.

Our department is committed to pushing students beyond the rote memory or "simply rehearse what others have said" syndromes to create their own expressions of biblical truth.

High Expectations. The Biblical Studies Department has a reputation on the Grace College campus for being a thought-provoking and demanding program. We are committed to excellence. Our students have done remarkably well in graduate schools and seminaries across the country. The faculty seek to model high expectations in their own performance as instructors. These expectations are manifested in the texts, projects, and level of interaction fostered by our department.

Study in Depth. One way an in-depth study is demonstrated is through our requirement that students have two years of a foreign language. Many of our majors take Greek and/or Hebrew, which allows them to read the biblical text in the original languages. The level of research required for assigned papers, as well as class discussions, gives students opportunities to interact on a deeper level.

Many students have grown up knowing a host of stories in the Bible. We attempt to encourage them to rethink many of those stories from multiple perspectives and to become aware that they address the deeper issues shared by all humankind. Our survey courses, rather than running lightly through the whole Bible, take select passages and treat them in depth. This is done to demonstrate to our students a methodology for going deeper and also to foster thinking at those levels.

Stewardship Toward Creation. In the creation account, man was given care of the garden, and even after the fall, man's struggle with the earth was apparent. At the other end of the spectrum, the future kingdom is portrayed in terms which envision the restoration of the earth. Since the creation reflects the work and character of God, it should not be defiled or abused. These principles are taught in discussions in class and also by the various recycling programs on this campus.

Conclusion

The Biblical Studies program plays a foundational role at Grace College. The school and its faculty are committed to teaching the Bible as God's inspired, inerrant word.

In a day in which morality is fading, the Bible stands as a pillar of that which is right, just, and loving. God's Word provides our students with a rock upon which to stand as they explore and evaluate various aspects of thought, life, and vocation. Our students take four required courses in this area, but this is not enough. The Bible's teachings are integrated into every area of study and co-curricular activities at Grace College.

The Biblical Studies Department is committed to the 13 values, and faculty members attempt by instruction, discussion, and modeling to implement these values into their own lives and into the lives of Grace College students.

Chapter 11

Communication

In the Christian Liberal Arts Curriculum

by Allyn P. Decker, Chairman
Communication Department

It is no accident that in the reception area of the Grace College Communication Department's offices there is a framed poster containing the question, "What Can I do With a Communication Degree?" Displayed around this question are the titles of more than 100 job titles ranging from "Disc Jockey" to "Stock Broker" to "City Transportation Coordinator." The point is this: one can do virtually anything with a communication degree.

At Grace College, we firmly believe that a major in Communication is extremely versatile and practical. Because the major contains emphases in general communication (speech, interpersonal communication, organizational communication, etc.); performance (oral interpretation, acting, directing, reader's theater, etc.); and mass media (public relations, broadcasting, etc.), the student can receive a wide variety of experiences applicable to virtually any career choice.

Other departments, such as Business and Behavioral Science, find our major extremely compatible with their disciplines. In fact, we have a number of students who double major because the courses are so complimentary.

Even more important is the way the department's curriculum dovetails with the whole liberal arts experience. It is not difficult at all to see each of the 13 institutional values integrated in the study of communication.

Educational Values

Shared Biblical Value. As the original "Great Communicator," Christ continually taught the importance of monitoring one's words and actions. He used dramatic story-telling to teach important lessons, and He commissioned a new generation of messengers to "go and tell. . ." This mandate is carried out through training in devotional, instructional, and persuasive speaking. Drama is a powerful form for telling the gospel; classes such as Religious Drama Workshop focus specifically on new ways to package and present the good news.

Critical Insight. "Making skillful judgments as to truth and merit" is a life-long activity that can be greatly enhanced through academic experience with courses such as Argumentation and Debate, Introduction to Mass Media, and Persuasion. Although we strive to use critical thinking in every course in the discipline, these three focus on this activity.

In addition, the department is currently sponsoring a lecture series entitled "Christians and Controversy." Guest speakers provide food for thought on current social, religious, and political issues. By its very title, our philosophy is made clear—good thinking begins with exposure to new ideas, and new ideas must always be put through the grid of good thinking.

Community Involvement. The study of theater and drama falls within the domain of the Communication Department. Through the production of plays and musicals, we are able to offer the community high-quality educational entertainment. Performance classes such as Reader's Theater, Directing, and Fundamentals of Acting also provide opportunities for public performances of students' work.

Each of our majors is encouraged to engage in some kind of applied study. This can be in the form of a creative project that incorporates classroom skills (e.g. developing a promotional video for a community agency, directing children's theater, or acting in educational theater groups). Alternatively, the experience may be gained as an intern for a local radio station, public relations firm, or advertising agency.

Students are always encouraged to investigate and report on current issues of local concern. Advanced speech students are required to do so, and they find this assignment most valuable.

Literacy. The study and practice of literature, effective speaking, and clear writing constitute the essence of an effective communication curriculum. Students learn the value of expressive oral interpretation of all genres of literature: poetry, prose, drama, humor, and Scripture. For students of public speaking, organization and outlining skills are of extreme importance, as is the dynamic delivery of one's message. Care is taken to help students know why a speech or a piece of literature is technically sound, but not to the point where the sheer pleasure of speaking, reading, or writing is overlooked.

Students also are taught the art of active listening in interpersonal, small group, and public communication encounters. Students evaluate one another's performances and must listen well in order to provide specific and constructive feedback.

Understanding Numerical Data. Within the discipline, a course in research methods is offered. Students learn how to conduct field studies, the scientific method is utilized, and laboratory findings are interpreted.

Numerical data in the form of facts and statistics are absolutely necessary as supporting material for one's thesis in written essays, speeches, and debates. Students are taught how to interpret and use data correctly and how to put large and impersonal numbers into perspective. The construction of effective visual aids hinges on one's ability to make sense out of statistical data.

Historical Consciousness. The course entitled American Public Address provides the opportunity for students to use rhetorical criticism and to catch a glimpse of the impact that public speech has had throughout American history. Great speakers such as Franklin D. Roosevelt, Martin Luther King Jr., and Ronald Reagan are studied in terms of content, speaking technique, and the significance of their messages to their times.

Scientific Understanding. The scientific method is taught and used in generating and interpreting data. Recent scientific discoveries in medicine, genetics, archaeology, and physics are the stuff of which good presentations are made. Course content in Broadcasting, Radio, and Video Production relies on scientific information in such fields as engineering, physics, and electronics.

Appreciation of the Fine Arts. As a member of the Fine Arts Division, the Communication Department works closely with the Music and Art Departments in the production of the college's spring musical. We also encourage students to express their artistic talents in set design and construction, make-up and costume design, and other theater crafts. Other activities include attendance at professional theater productions and art galleries. A well constructed and delivered speech requires a certain amount of artistry as well. Verbal symmetry, word coloring, and physical expression are necessary for vivid speaking.

International, Multi-Cultural Awareness. Students are taught the cultural uniqueness of non-verbal communication (i.e. what is an acceptable expression or gesture in our culture may be considered offensive in other parts of the world). As students analyze audiences for public communication, they are also taught to consider cultural, ethnical, and socio-economic differences. Many of our students are considering careers in missions or youth ministry and often use their summers to tour or serve in foreign countries.

Creativity. Communication studies celebrate creativity! Whether the student is generating a speech, preparing a monologue, suggesting changes for a social policy, or generally searching for newer, fresher ways to communicate his or her ideas to others, creativity is being used. In the recent past, students have embraced new technologies in communication and have used them very effectively. Camcorders, video still cameras, and computer-generated graphics bring a creative energy to presentations.

High Expectations. Advanced courses in public communication, debate, and acting are all performance-oriented. Just enough theory is given for competency, and the rest of the course is spent learning by doing. Minimum competency levels are established in each course, and because students in many of these courses perform for the general student public, they feel the pressure of maintaining high standards. Performances are often videotaped and consequently provide objective visual feedback.

Study In Depth. Because our discipline embraces the arts, humanities, and social sciences, we are afforded the challenging (and sometimes overwhelming) task of studying human issues. As students grapple with the physical, social, sexual, and spiritual nature of humans, deeper issues automatically emerge. Students are given the necessary resources to investigate these issues: interviews with community leaders or local experts, written material from departmental and college libraries, and help from teaching assistants who can be the "arms and legs" for professors who would like to, but cannot, be accessible to every student. Not only are the resources provided, but also students are granted a public forum for their ideas. Communication courses fully acknowledge the right and responsibility of the freedom of speech.

Stewardship Toward Creation. The average college student is just beginning to recognize the frightening plight of our environment. Along with this recognition comes the need to examine one's own stewardship—or lack of it. Effective action comes from examining the issues, and this is what we encourage through speech and drama. The communication discipline mirrors society and can also shape it. Through compelling communication, available in a variety of forms, the student can expose problems and offer solutions. Usually that begins with campus examples of wastefulness or abuse and extends outward to the larger society.

Pursuing these institutional values within the framework of communication studies is invigorating and rewarding. The reader has seen that the potential for accomplishing these values is well within the student's reach. As faculty members, we strive to keep these ideals foremost in our minds and offer the most valuable experiences possible.

Appendices

Appendix 1

The 13 Values

The mission of Grace College is to help equip students to make fruitful contact with God's world and to convert that knowledge into productive and redemptive work in the world. As the college's curricular and extra-curricular activities involve themselves with these values, we believe our mission will be fulfilled. Ours is a value-driven curriculum. We believe these values to be theologically grounded and philosophically and educationally sound.

1. *Shared Biblical Value*: Students should be guaranteed a purposeful and structured opportunity to work out and implement individually and corporately the biblical presentation of the redeemed life in all spheres of God's creation.

   A person who has had exposure to this value will:

   A. comprehend and accept that biblical theology is more than a set of doctrines to be believed; it is a whole fabric to be woven into a spirit which is demonstrated in one's lifestyle.

B. learn about, develop, and describe the fabric of values intrinsic to the historic Christian faith, the most preeminent being redemption and its holistic implications.

C. become a practitioner of the redeemed life with regard to the physical creation, personal self and family, human society and condition, and corporate church life.

2. *Critical Insight*: Students should be guaranteed a structured opportunity to develop abilities to make skillful judgments as to truth and merit.

A person who has had exposure to this value will:

A. improve one's thinking capabilities by becoming aware of how one thinks; i.e. to develop the ability to think about thinking.

B. develop and sharpen skills for discerning intents, assumptions, values, biases, methods, rhetorical features, and propagandistic techniques in everything read, heard, or viewed.

C. discern, follow, and analyze the merit of the progression of argumentation as well as assess the truth and merit of conclusions.

D. have heightened sensitivities to historical and contemporary ethical dilemmas by becoming able to discern, describe, and summarize the nature of the problems and the values which underwrite them.

E. confront the issues, assess the multiplicity of competing perspectives, and draw satisfactory conclusions or learn to live with the ambiguities which are intrinsic to some matters.

F. develop the ability for principled reflective thinking about oneself, one's place in the world, and the most appropriate application of the values of the Kingdom of Christ to the world.

3. *Community Involvement*: Students should be guaranteed opportunity for structured exchanges with the community's social, economic, political, cultural, and religious life; through this means students can have positive experiences in applying values and skills to the realities of human society.

   A person who has had exposure to this value will:

   A. demonstrate knowledge about the traditions, governmental units, services, and purposes of a community.

   B. actively participate in the economic, social, political, cultural, and religious elements within the community.

   C. interface one's Christian values and belief system with the community in which one is involved.

4. *Literacy—Writing, Reading, Speaking, Listening*: Students should be guaranteed a structured opportunity to grasp a functional knowledge of the English language and to be proficient in writing accurately and expressively without flaws in mechanics, usage, or organization. In reading . . . to comprehend any non-technical material in English, including major works of literature, and to do so at the national average of 250 wpm or better. In speaking, to express ideas with force and clarity, and discuss on a principled level the various areas and issues of life. In listening . . . to become a critical consumer of media and other modes of expression, and be able to discriminate slanted or propagandistic material.

A person who has had exposure to this value will use the four components of communication (reading, writing, speaking, and listening) in an ongoing process of learning. This means the person will:

A. read a breadth of literature at an appropriate rate and comprehend various literary genre.

B. put one's ideas into an accurate and logically structured written form free of grammatical errors.

C. put one's ideas into an accurate and logically structured speech and be able to deliver it confidently and effectively to any specified audience.

D. listen critically, being able to respond accurately and logically concerning what was heard and being able to recognize slanted or propagandistic material.

E. use the skills of literacy to spread the message of the gospel of the Kingdom of Christ.

5. *Understanding Numerical Data*: Students should be guaranteed a structured opportunity to grasp the power and limitation of mathematics and to develop a critical understanding of published data including graphs and statistical results.

A person who has had exposure to this value will:

A. understand the basic structures, operations, and properties of mathematics.

B. relate mathematical functions to their specific graphical representations.

C. use mathematical functions, operations, and properties to describe God's creation.

6. *Historical Consciousness*: Students should be guaranteed a structured opportunity to understand and appreciate the contributions of earlier civilizations, the reality that all are products of time and culture, and the origins and meanings of Christian Theism.

A person who has had exposure to this value will:

A. identify the significant eras, central events, great personalities, and agents of change in the past and assess the impact these have on contemporary and will have on future social, legal, political, economic, and religious features of history.

B. imaginatively recreate the past and inquire about its conditions, complexities, and options, and assess the results of these choices both in individual and societal ways.

C. identify and explore the role of the providence of God in the supervision of the flow of history.

D. discern and appreciate that Christian Theism is a historical religion grounded in certain identifiable historical events.

E. explore and make use of how the present has been influenced by the past, by creating a vision of one's role in using the present to further the Kingdom of Christ.

7. *Scientific Understanding—Method, Meaning, History*: Students should be guaranteed a structured opportunity to experience the breadth, meaning, and application of the physical/biological sciences in our culture and to do so from a biblical worldview.

A person who has had exposure to this value will:

A. recognize how scientific reasoning has been and is being used in the development of concepts and principles in science.

B. be able to extend one's senses through instrumentation in the process of studying God's creation.

C. use existing standards of measure or develop appropriate new operationally defined ones.

D. evaluate the impact of science on society and of society on science.

E. use scientific reasoning in structured and unstructured experiences for the purpose of understanding and describing God's creation.

F. explore what impact scientific reasoning has for the service of mankind.

8. *Appreciation of the Fine Arts*: Students should be guaranteed a structured opportunity to develop a sensitivity in making artistic judgments about what is seen and heard through exposure to fine arts; this sensitivity will enable students to evaluate their own aesthetic choices and those of others.

A person who has had exposure to this value will:

A. demonstrate an appreciation of the arts by regular interaction with artistic expressions.

B. recognize different styles and types of artistic expression and identify their particular era or culture.

C. identify influences contributing to the creative expressions of others and the impact of creative expressions on culture.

D. recognize how various art forms are used to communicate ideas.

E. develop the skills necessary to make appropriate artistic judgments about what is seen and heard, and to hone one's own aesthetic choices.

F. give creative expression in behalf of the Kingdom of Christ.

9. *International, Multi-Cultural Awareness*: Students should be guaranteed a structured opportunity to be inducted into a cultural experience outside their own through foreign language study, study abroad, inner-city and mission-station ministries, and cross-cultural courses.

A person who has had exposure to this value will:

A. compare his or her culture with other dissimilar cultures, highlighting economic, political, religious, and social differences and similarities.

B. analyze other cultures, citing the strengths and weaknesses of their economic, political, religious, and social systems.

C. demonstrate an appreciation of and respect for the economic, political, religious, and social differences that are characteristic of cultures different from one's own.

D. have a firsthand encounter with a culture dissimilar from one's own, and analyze and describe the distinctives of that culture.

10. *Creativity*: Students should be guaranteed enough freedom from conformity, censorship, regimentation, and the urge for quick solutions so that each task may include the opportunity to discover new or improved solutions to problems.

    A person who has had exposure to this value will:

    A. critique existing solutions, citing their strengths and weaknesses.

    B. pose new solutions to existing problems.

    C. develop the capacity for creative theorizing and problem solving when encountering issues which are new or for which there are no previously developed conclusions.

11. *High Expectations*: Students should be guaranteed that they will be expected in every case to achieve institutionally identified minimum competencies in all general education areas and to explore the maximum of their potential.

    A person who has had exposure to this value will:

    A. understand that the privilege of studying at the college level requires that one responsibly contribute to the society in which one is a member.

    B. explore the characteristics of excellence and cultivate a continuing commitment to achieve it in every activity of life.

C. push oneself beyond one's present perceived capabilities, identifying ways to empower oneself to address significant issues and make substantial contributions to society.

D. explore and develop an improved sense of self and one's role in the compelling vision of the Kingdom of Christ as one becomes empowered to exceed the minimum and rise above the ordinary.

12. *Study in Depth*: Students should be guaranteed the opportunity, time, and institutional resources to grapple in depth with significant human problems in order to stretch their capacities for insight and solution.

    A person who has had exposure to this value will:

    A. investigate significant human issues utilizing appropriate research tools one has accumulated.

    B. express in a meaningful way the results of one's research.

    C. participate in interdisciplinary investigations which lead to proposed solutions.

    D. synthesize the various elements of one's college experience into a meaningful expression of the compelling vision of the Kingdom of Christ.

13. *Stewardship Toward Creation*: Students should be guaranteed an experience in acting as stewards of God's creation

so that they witness the impacts of environmental care and abuse.

A person who has had exposure to this value will:

A. explore the multiple dimensions of the relationships within the ecosystem.

B. analyze examples of environmental management for care and for abuse of the ecosystem in order to identify personal stewardship values.

C. explore Christian principles guiding the practice of stewardship within the ecosystem.

D. participate in an environmental issue which leads toward identification of:

   1) the complex and competing interests and values at work.

   2) processes for bringing positive change.

   3) a Christian response to the issue.

   4) a map of structured activities to actualize positive change in the ecosystem.

E. actualize positive change in the ecosystem by completing activities outlined in the map of activities (D, 4 above).

Appendix 2

Programs of Study

Grace College offers 50 majors, minors, and specializations in its Christian liberal arts curriculum. All students complete core general education studies, as well as the curriculum in their area of academic emphasis. In every area, curricula have been designed to incorporate the 13 educational values described in Appendix 1 as the driving force.

Areas of study at Grace College are:

- Accounting
- Art
- Art Education
- Biblical Studies
- Biblical Languages*
- Biology
- Biology Education
- Business Administration
- Business Education
- Christian Ministries
- Communication

- Computer Science*
- Counseling
- Criminal Justice
- Education–Elementary
- Education–Secondary
- English
- English Education
- French
- French Education
- General Science
- German
- German Education
- Graphic Arts
- International Business
- Journalism*
- Journalism Education
- Linguistics
- Mathematics
- Mathematics Education
- Music–Applied (Performance)
- Music Education
- Music Management
- Pedagogy*
- Physical Education
- Physical Education–Teaching (All-Grade)
- Physical Education–Teaching (Secondary)
- Pre-Dentistry
- Pre-Law
- Pre-Medicine
- Pre-Pharmacy
- Pre-Physical Therapy
- Pre-Veterinary Medicine
- Psychology

- Russian
- Science Education–Secondary
- Sociology
- Spanish
- Spanish Education
- Special Education–L.D.*

* Indicates minor only.

Appendix 3

Covenant of Faith

Paragraph VI of Grace College's charter states one of the essential purposes of Grace College: "To carry on the educational activities of this corporation in complete harmony with the articles of the following 'Covenant of Faith,' which cannot be changed or diminished." Each member of the college's faculty and Board of Trustees subscribes annually in writing to the Covenant of Faith.

Grace College Covenant of Faith

1. *We believe in THE HOLY SCRIPTURES:* accepting fully the writings of the Old and New Testaments as the very Word of God, verbally inspired in all parts and therefore wholly without error as originally given of God, altogether sufficient in themselves as our only infallible rule of faith and practice (Matt. 5:18; John 10:35; 16:13; 17:17; 2 Tim. 3:16; 2 Peter 1:21).

2. *We believe in THE ONE TRIUNE GOD:* who is personal, spirit, and sovereign (Mark 12:29; John 4:24; 14:9; Ps. 135:6);

perfect, infinite, and eternal in His being, holiness, love, wisdom, and power (Ps. 18:30, 147:5; Deut. 33:27); absolutely separate and above the world as its Creator, yet everywhere present in the world as the Upholder of all things (Gen. 1:1; Ps. 104); self-existent and self-revealing in three distinct Persons—the Father, the Son, and the Holy Spirit (John 5:26; Matt. 28:19; 2 Cor. 13:14), each of whom is to be honored and worshipped equally as true God (John 5:23; Acts 5:3-4).

3. *We believe in THE LORD JESUS CHRIST:* who is the Second Person of the Triune God, the eternal Word and Only Begotten Son, our great God and Savior (John 1:1; 3:16; Titus 2:13; Rom 9:5); that, without any essential change in His divine Person (Heb. 13:8), He became man by the miracle of virgin birth (John 1:14; Matt. 1:23), thus to continue forever as both true God Man, one Person with two natures (Col. 2:9; Rev. 22:16); that as Man, He was in all points tempted like as we are, yet without sin (Heb. 4:15; John 8:46); that as the perfect Lamb of God He gave Himself in death upon the cross, bearing there the sin of the world and suffering its full penalty of divine wrath in our stead (Isa. 53:5-6; Matt. 20:28; Gal. 3:13; John 1:29); that He arose again from the dead and was glorified in the same body in which He suffered and died (Luke 24:36-43; John 20:25-28); that as our great High Priest He ascended into heaven, there to appear before the face of God as our Advocate and Intercessor (Heb. 4:14; 9:24; 1 John 2:1).

4. *We believe in THE HOLY SPIRIT:* who is the Third Person of the Triune God (Matt. 28:19; Acts 5:3-4), the divine Agent in nature, revelation, and redemption (Gen. 1:2; Ps. 104:30; 1 Cor. 2:10; 2 Cor. 3:18); that He convicts the world of sin (John 16:8-11), regenerates those who believe (John 3:5), and indwells, baptizes, seals, empowers, guides, teaches, and sanctifies all

who become children of God through Christ (1 Cor. 6:19; 12:13; Eph. 4:30; 3:16; Rom. 8:14; John 14:26; 1 Cor. 6:11).

5. *We believe in THE CREATION AND FALL OF MAN:* that he was the direct creation of God, spirit and soul and body, not in any sense the product of an animal ancestry, but made in the divine image (Gen. 1:26-29; 2:7 and 18:24; Matt. 19:4; 1 Thess. 5:23); that by personal disobedience to the revealed will of God, man became a sinful creature and the progenitor of a fallen race (Gen. 3:1-24; 5:3), who are universally sinful in both nature and practice (Eph. 2:3; Rom. 3:23; 5:12), alienated from the life and family of God (Eph. 4:18; John 8:42-44), under the righteous judgment and wrath of God (Rom. 1:18; 3:19), and have within themselves no possible means of recovery or salvation (Mark 7:21-23; Matt. 19:26; Rom. 7:18).

6. *We believe in SALVATION BY GRACE THROUGH FAITH:* that salvation is the free gift of God (Rom. 3:24; 6:23), neither merited nor secured in part or in whole by any virtue of work of man (Titus 3:5; Rom. 4:4-5; 11:16), but received only by personal faith in the Lord Jesus Christ (John 3:16, 6:28-29; Acts 16:30-31; Eph. 2:8-9), in whom all true believers have as a present possession the gift of eternal life, a perfect righteousness, sonship in the family of God, deliverance and security from all condemnation, every spiritual resource needed for life and godliness, and the divine guarantee that they shall never perish (1 John 5:13; Rom. 3:22; Gal. 3:26; John 5:24; Eph 1:3; 2 Peter 1:3; John 10:27-30); that this salvation includes the whole man, spirit and soul and body (1 Thess. 5:23-24); and apart from Christ there is no possible salvation (John 14:6; Acts 4:12).

7. *We believe in RIGHTEOUS LIVING AND GOOD WORKS:* not as the procuring cause of salvation in any sense, but as its

proper evidence and fruit (1 John 3:9-11; 4:19; 5:4; Eph. 2:8-10; Titus 2:14; Matt. 7:16-18; 1 Cor. 15:10); and therefore as Christians we should keep the word of our Lord (John 14:23), seek the things which are above (Col. 3:1), walk as He walked (1 John 2:6), be careful to maintain good works (Titus 3:8), and especially accept as our solemn responsibility the duty and privilege of bearing the Gospel to a lost world in order that we may bear much fruit (Acts 1:8; 2 Cor. 5:19; John 15:16); remembering that a victorious and fruitful Christian life is possible only for those who have learned that they are not under law but under grace (Rom. 6:14), and who in gratitude for the infinite and undeserved mercies of God have presented themselves wholly to Him for His service (Rom. 12:1-2).

8. *We believe in THE EXISTENCE OF SATAN:* who originally was created a holy and perfect being, but through pride and unlawful ambition rebelled against God (Ezek. 18:13-17; Isa. 14:13-14; 1 Tim. 3:7); thus becoming utterly depraved in character (John 8:44), the great Adversary of God and His people (Matt. 4:1-11; Rev. 12:10), leader of all other evil angels and spirits (Matt. 12:24-26; 25:41), the deceiver and god of this present world (Rev. 12:9; 2 Cor. 4:4); that his powers are supernaturally great, but strictly limited by the permissive will of God, who overrules all his wicked devices for good (Job 1:1-22; Luke 22:31-32); that he was defeated and judged at the cross, and therefore his final doom is certain (John 12:31-32; 16:11; Rev. 20:10); that we are able to resist and overcome him only in the armor of God and by the Blood of the Lamb (Eph. 6:12-18; Rev. 12:11).

9. *We believe in THE SECOND COMING OF CHRIST:* that His return from heaven will be personal, visible, and glorious—a Blessed Hope for which we should constantly

watch and pray, the time being unrevealed but always imminent (Acts 1:11; Rev. 1:7; Mark 13:33-37; Titus 2:11-13; Rev. 22:20); that when He comes He will first by resurrection and translation remove from the earth His waiting Church (1 Thess. 4:16-18), then pour out the righteous judgments of God upon the unbelieving world (Rev. 6:1-18:24), afterward descend with His church and establish His glorious and literal kingdom over all the nations for a thousand years (Rev. 19:1-20:6; Matt. 13:41-43), at the close of which He will rise and judge the unsaved dead (Rev. 20:11-15), and finally as the Son of David deliver up His Messianic Kingdom to God the Father (1 Cor. 15:24-28), in order that as the Eternal Son He may reign forever with the Father in the New Heaven and the New Earth (Luke 1:32-33; Rev. 21:1-22:6).

10. We believe in FUTURE LIFE, BODILY RESURRECTION, AND ETERNAL JUDGMENT: that the spirits of the saved at death go immediately to be with Christ in heaven (Phil. 1:21-23; 2 Cor. 5:8), where they abide in joyful fellowship with Him until His second coming, when their bodies shall be raised from the grave and changed into the likeness of His own glorious body (Phil. 3:20-21; 1 Cor. 15:35-58; 1 John 3:2), at which time their works shall be brought before the Judgment Seat of Christ for the determination of rewards, a judgment which may issue in the loss of rewards, but not in the loss of the soul (1 Cor. 3:8-15); that the spirits of the unsaved at death descend immediately into Hades where they are kept under punishment until the final day of judgment (Luke 16:19-31; 2 Peter 2:9), at which time their bodies shall be judged according to their works and cast into the place of final and everlasting punishment (Rev. 20:11-15; 21:8; Mark 9:43-48; Jude 13).

11. *We believe in THE ONE TRUE CHURCH:* the mystical Body and Bride of the Lord Jesus (Eph. 4:4; 5:25-32), which He began to build on the day of Pentecost (Matt. 16:18; Acts 2:47), and will complete at His second coming (1 Thess. 4:16-17); and into which all true believers of the present age are baptized immediately by the Holy Spirit (1 Cor. 12:12-13 with 1:2); that all the various members of this one spiritual Body should assemble themselves together in local churches for worship, prayer, fellowship, teaching, united testimony, and the observance of the ordinances of our Lord (Heb. 10:25; Acts 2:41-47), among which are the following: the baptism of believers by triune immersion (Matt. 28:20), the laying on of hands (1 Tim. 4:14; 2 Tim. 1:6), the washing of the saints' feet (John 13:1-17), the Lord's Supper or Lovefeast (1 Cor. 11:17-22; Jude 12), the Communion of the bread and cup (1 Cor. 11:23-24), and prayer and anointing for the sick (James 5:13-18).

12. *We believe in SEPARATION FROM THE WORLD:* that since our Christian citizenship is in heaven, as the children of God we should walk in separation from this present world, having no fellowship with its evil ways (Phil. 3:20: 2 Cor. 6:14-18; Rom. 12:2; Eph. 5:11), abstaining from all worldly amusements and unclean habits which defile mind and body (Luke 8:14; 1 Thess. 5:22; 1 Tim. 5:6; 1 Peter 2:11; Eph. 5:3-11, 18; Col. 3:17; 1 Cor. 6:19-20), from the sin of divorce and remarriage as forbidden by our Lord (Matt. 19:9), from the swearing of any oath (James 5:12), from the use of unbelieving courts for the settlement of disputes between Christians (1 Cor. 6:1-9), and from taking personal vengeance in carnal strife (Rom. 12:18-21; 2 Cor. 10:3-4).